College IS for Lunkheads

What's Wrong With College

The American Dream Turned Nightmare

Expelling the Myths of a College Education

Frank Don

East West College Counseling LLLP
370 Golfview Road, Suite 801
North Palm Beach, Florida 33408

frankdonew@gmail.com

LIBRARY OF CONGRESS CATALOGING-IN-PUBLICATION DATA

ISBN 978-1-7334024-0-8
ISBN 978-1-7334024-1-5   (ebook)

CONTENTS

PREFACE

The American Dream! How often have we heard that phrase? The American Dream has brought people from the four corners of the world in search of the promised land.

The United States was referred to as the New Jerusalem, a land of opportunity. Tales were told of streets paved with gold. There were no limitations, only opportunities. Or so it was told.

The American Dream was a land of plenty--- a bounty of food, a wealth of job opportunities and possible riches beyond compare. And the American Dream was available to anyone who was industrious and worked hard.

Times change, and with it a sense that to have a slice of the American Dream Pie it was not good enough just to work hard. No, with changing times came changing needs. One essential need was an education and not just an elementary school education or a high school education. No, the times demanded a college education in order to get a good job, make a good salary and to be able to fully embrace the American Dream.

And so it was told. A college education became a necessity.
And so it was believed. And so by many it continues to be
believed to be so.

But is it? Is it really so?

Is the college education of today worth the investment in
time and money, debt taken on and income deferred that we
are told it is?

Some people would point to statistics to make the case that a
college education is the basis for an increased income
differential compared to those without such an education.

As I will address and indicate, today's college education may
just be BS --- not a B.S. as in bachelor of sciences degree ---
but bs as in the proverbial bullshit.

Instead of opening doors of opportunity, today's college
education can be a costly piece of paper that indentures the
student to a heavy debt load for years to come. A college
degree today may provide nothing more than a piece of
paper that holds no value in the short-term or possibly either
in the long-term.

the times they are a'changing

A college education may have been a door opener in years
past, not so much in today's environment and perhaps even
less so in the unfolding conditions of the future economy.

I know in what I write I have jarred some people from their belief system. Like a whack on the side of the head, I may have clobbered you.   For many, I sound like a heretic denouncing the American way.

But this way, this belief in the importance of college education as it is presently formulated, is no longer the highway to a better life. On the contrary, it is a road with speed bumps, potholes and possibly leading across the bridge to nowhere.

I acknowledge at the inception of this book that I am spitting into the wind. I recognize that my view may be perceived as nothing more than a contrarian perspective.

But I also realize that someone, and some people, must pierce the veil of illusion related to a college education in today's world.

Not only does today's higher education no longer serve a truly useful purpose. Today's education subtly enslaves the individual student --- enslaves the individual in the conditioning of the mind into a societal consensus and enslaves the individual in the financial obligations of student loan debt and consequently places restrictions on future choices of the individual. Options and alternatives become limited, all thanks to a promise that has neither heart nor soul.

As it was once formulated, college education had a real purpose and significant meaning. But purpose and meaning of the college degree became lost as education turned its focus and adapted a wrong focus. Join me as I share my thoughts, explain my reasoning and discuss how today's college education could lead students on a race to nowhere…

THE PREMISE

Post-secondary education of college or university has been a part of the American mindset since the colonial days, long before the American Revolution and long before the United States established itself as an independent nation.

The first college in the US was Harvard College founded by the colonial legislature in 1636 and modeled after the English universities of Oxford and Cambridge. While much of the founding sentiment was to

'advance learning and perpetuate it to posterity'

the primary goal was the training of young men for the ministry to succeed the established ministers who would eventually pass on.

Later, college education would be the training ground for lawyers, politicians and planters. But the focus continued to be on training young men for the ministry. Those students were often given free tuition.

Various colleges sprang up, but most of the early colleges were devoted to the training of ministers according to their particular religious denomination.

In growing dissatisfaction with the liberal theology of Harvard,

Conservative Puritan ministers founded Yale.

Presbyterians established the College of New Jersey, later renamed Princeton University.

Baptists established Rhode Island College, later renamed Brown University.

The Anglicans established King's College, later renamed Columbia University.

The Dutch Reform Church established Queen's College, later renamed Rutgers University.

It was not until 1749 when Benjamin Franklin and other Philadelphia leaders created the Academy of Pennsylvania that a college education was no longer focused on the training for a ministry. This school would eventually be renamed in 1791 as the University of Pennsylvania.

Students at colleges were young men primarily from the upper classes of society, the *elite* members of society.

It is interesting to note how strong the influence of religiosity was on the founding of post-secondary education in the United States.

While higher education primarily favored the *elite*, a movement developed in the US to provide practical higher education to the general populace.

In 1862, the US Congress passed the Morrill Land-Grant Colleges Act, the beginning of government funded, public universities. Concentrated in the western US states initially, the Morrill Act made higher education more accessible to the citizenry. Eventually, the Act was extended to include all states, and today every state has some form of a public university.

A major purpose of the Morrill Act was to provide higher education to its citizens of a

practical application

specifically in agriculture and engineering. These public colleges were to provide formal education in *"agriculture, home economics, mechanical arts, and other professions that seemed practical at the time."*

By 1897, the number of higher education institutions in the US reached 821, up from 23 in 1800.

Even from the very beginning, college education in the United States was geared towards *'career'* education, a mindset that continues today and raises the issues of whether the hype of college as an education to develop the character and intellect of the student is but a veil to the true purpose of *'career'* education, molding the student into the most appropriate patterns for a worker bee.

Certainly, the much-ballyhooed justification of college education as ROI [return on investment] emphasizes the work / job / career focus over the growth and development of the student's character, maturity, intellect and critical thinking.

While the individual tenets of different denominations of religiosity of early college education may have dropped away, the mindset of specific philosophical outlooks seems to continue.

Students may no longer have to wear the ministerial robes in college, but they may have to parrot a *"preach to the choir"* attitude to be successful in their college career.

The attributes of critical thinking whereby the individual considers both the thesis and antithesis to arrive at an even more enlightened synthesis are rarely engaged in higher education today. Instead, the philosophical mindset of the professor, teacher, teacher's aid often limit the transmission of information and call for a reaffirmation of that particular facilitator's belief system by the student who wishes to excel.

Is this higher education?

I would suggest not. Rather, it is merely the continuation of rote and regurgitation of certain precepts backed by the constrained evidence to solely support one's thesis.

We have to ask ourselves: what is the true purpose of higher education? What is the meaning of going for a college education in the larger picture of one's success in life?

And not success solely judged on material success but success in self-fulfillment, self-realization --- the whole enchilada of life's journey.

The promise of post-secondary education offers something far greater than a mere career education based on a variable R-O-I [return on investment].

THE PROMISE

Similar to human growth and development itself --- on a physical, emotional and psychological level --- education also grows and develops in accord with the individual's maturation and character development.

In the early stages of education, elementary school, children have the opportunity to learn the basics --- once referred to as the three r's of reading, writing and arithmetic. The fundamental skills of learning are taught, and children become proficient in the basics of education.

As the child develops, the mind grows more inquisitive.

Education should provide a stretch of the adolescent's mind, allowing the child to explore, investigate and discover varied aspects of life and his or her own character.

The foundation stones are set in elementary school education. As the child develops physically, emotionally and intellectually, so too does the focus of education. There is a widening of scope, a move beyond merely learning the basics into delving deeper into subject matter.

As the child becoming young adult looks to the adult for reinforcement and approval, there is a tendency for the middle school student to parrot much of the thought and beliefs of their teacher, their facilitator.

Trust is often bestowed upon the teacher, and in times past and in some countries still today, the teacher was a venerated position --- a position of respect and great responsibility. The teacher was the steward of the intellectual development of the young person. And the student would seek the praise of the teacher, most often done by the student giving to the teacher what the teacher expected of the student.

High school becomes a time when the student develops their critical thinking, finds their voice, and draws upon various outlets for their individual expression.

This is the phase of education when the student like a baby bird tests their wings, stretches into their personal identity but all with the safety net of their structured school in their local community with support from teachers, parents and friends.

College is seen as a time when the young adult grows into greater independence, given the responsibility and accountability for making personal decisions, provided the opportunity to devise one's own academic curriculum and to live their lives free of overbearing adult supervision.

College was a time in which the young adult could grow ever more into adulthood, develop a greater self-identity and explore the many options to create the foundation stones of their future.

So it was promised… but a promise that has become tainted and even toxic to the true growth of the individuality, the full development of self-identity, and even the unrestricted tool set for their future.

The college experience of the past is not the college experience of the present.

Promises have gone unfulfilled and on the contrary the promise of college has become a bitter taste for many.

And so we look at higher education and must raise the question: What's Wrong With College?

Chapter 1:   SLAYING THE GOLDEN CALF

Unless you've had your head under a rock over the past few years, you've heard it, read about it, might even have discussed it with other people.

And if you have a child heading off to college, have a child in college, or are a college student yourself, you know it all too well.

College costs over recent times have exploded. Tuition and college fees and ancillary costs can run as much as $60,000+ a year. For a four-year college degree, you could be seeing a college degree price tag as high as $240,000 or more.

And who says you can graduate nowadays in just four years when even colleges are suggesting that it may take 5-6 years to graduate? According to the US Department of Education, only 54% of undergraduate students graduate within 6 years.

You must be kidding!

Since 1978, the costs for a college education have increased tenfold.

TENFOLD

Since 2000, the average cost of college has increased by 92%.

Has the cost of educating a student risen so exponentially? Or have other factors been at work to increase the cost of a college education?

I suggest the latter, and the statistics back up my contention.

One can make the case that the cost of educating a student has gone up, but by 92% or 1120%?

 I don't think so.

To pay for those college costs, students and their parents have taken on student loan debt.

DEBT

Student loan debt in the US is over 1.3 trillion dollars. Not a gazillion, but $1,300,000,000,000.

Approximately 10 million federal student loans are taken out annually.

6.7 million student loan borrowers who are in repayment process are delinquent.

And the one loan that is NOT forgiven in bankruptcy is student loans.

Talk about a squeeze on young adults who are only at the beginning of the salary cycle when they first graduate college!

Add to that the fact that the present interest rate on federal undergraduate student loans is 4.66% and for graduate students the loan rate is 6.2% and for parents borrowing through the PLUS program the rate is 7.2%... all the while that bank savings accounts are paying little more than .10% interest, and you have an almost obscene, virtually usury, interest rate placed upon students.

And for what?

I'll get into the *'for what'* later on, but let's follow this brambled path of college costs and see where it leads.

With the dramatic increase in the costs of a college education, we have to ask ourselves where does the money go?

We have all heard about the top 1% in our society making millions, even billions, in compensation for their *'efforts'* or, at least, for their position within the organization.

When one compares the salaries of college administrators to the salaries of college faculty, the discrepancy is staggering.

While faculty salaries will vary according to field of discipline, a tenured professor average salary is about $100,000. And tenure in today's college world is like the illusory pot of gold at the end of the rainbow.

Increasingly, colleges are staffing their classrooms with adjunct professors. Tenure is becoming a fading memory of the past higher education schema.

While the faculty seems to be largely stiffed, that is not the case for the college administration.

For a college President, the median earning is over $425,000 with some college presidents earning more than $1 million in their compensation package with some presidents earning over several million dollars.

Increasingly, we see education moving away from a profession into a business.

Like a business, higher education has become susceptible to imposed standards, regulations, and overweening monitoring of college and university principles and practices.

While colleges and universities tended to be more independent in times past, relationships with government and corporate entities have created a tangled web that demand higher education be compliant with various legal statutes and regulations.

Of the 6,760 colleges and universities in the US, there are only a small number who refuse to participate in federal financial-aid programs. Among the colleges and universities that do not participate in Title IV financial aid programs are:

- Hillsdale College in Michigan
- Grove City College in Pennsylvania
- Christendom College in Virginia
- Patrick Henry College in Virginia
- Pensacola Christian College in Florida

- Yeshiva Toras Chaim Talmudic Seminary in Colorado
- Wyoming Catholic College in Wyoming
- Gutenberg College in Oregon

The vast majority of colleges and universities offer federal financial-aid programs and with them come greater government regulatory and bureaucratic intrusion. With their tentacles into higher education, the government can make and enforce certain rules and regulations imposed upon higher education.

One such governmental regulation is Title IX that became law in June of 1972 and leveled the playing field for women in the academic and athletic realms of higher education.

Prior to the implementation of Title IX, women were not given the same opportunities that men were. Academic opportunities of scholarships and funding were offered to men but not to women, for women were not viewed as equal to men.

The intention of non-discrimination and righting past wrongs is a noble cause but as with any situation there are often collateral issues and unforeseen consequences.

With financial aid being provided students by the federal government, the federal government becomes a major stakeholder in each college and university and how that college or university performs both in regard to non-discrimination but also the school's effectiveness.

Once the government gets a toehold, it seems the government tries to get their foot further in the door.

From 1997 to 2012, federal regulations on higher education institutions rose by 56%. In order to ensure compliance with increasing governmental regulations, colleges and universities needed more administrative staff.

Government is not the only recent stakeholder in higher education with the ability to formulate policies for colleges and universities to enforce.

Another stakeholder in higher education and one that has been at the table for many years but whose presence and influence have increased since the late 1970's is Corporate Americana.

Our society is a consumer society with 70% of the US nation's GDP being the consumer. Ever since the end of the Second World War, the US has been on a consumption binge. Advertisers and marketers plant seeds within the consciousness of stuff for us to have, stuff for us to want and stuff for us to acquire.

Easy credit of recent years has allowed people to have it NOW. No longer do people have to wait and save until they have the monies available to buy that wanted thing. No, the individual consumer can have it now and pay for it over time on credit.

And who makes the stuff that we want? Corporations.

As we became increasingly aware of or subject to the dominance of business interests, colleges and universities saw opportunities. No longer did colleges and universities have to rely solely on donors, as they once did during the robber baron period or subsequently on the largesse of a wealthy benefactor.

Colleges could now use their resources in a vast array of commercial endeavors. With a shift from the Industrial Age [the manufacturing era] into the Information Age [the knowledge era], colleges and universities were well placed for money-making opportunities through research, knowledge and commercial development.

There are increasing projects that draw upon government, private enterprise and higher education or a combination of government and higher education or a combination of private corporations and higher education or a combination of all three.

Various research projects carried out at various universities are under the auspices of different federal government agencies.

In 2016 the US Department of Defense issued 23 awards to academic institutions for research totaling $162 million over five years.

That same year NASA awarded $8 million in grants for university research and development programs.

The National Institute of Health awards nearly $30 billion annually in medical research grants to colleges and universities, including medical schools and other research institutions.

26 Federal Agencies offer grants, and many of these grants go to colleges and universities. Some grants go to college students directly.

Talk about having skin in the game!

If an individual is receiving grant monies from a governmental agency, is that student likely to criticize that agency and its policies? Or is that student more likely to accept and accommodate where the money is coming from? It is rare for someone to bite the hand that feeds them.

And what about grants to higher education institutions? If a college or university is receiving US government assistance through grants, can it open the door to influence and impact on college or university policy?

Of course it can!

Government influence can be imposed either directly through certain rules and regulations stipulated in the grant, or government influence could be implicit recognizing that decisions made by college or university administrators would be impacted if not playing nice with the grant-making governmental agency.

You might assume that I'm being caustic in my assessment, but to think that all actions by government are altruistic is living in a fantasyland and not true reality. If you have the opportunity to influence policies and decisions, wouldn't there be times when you would exercise that influence? Of course you would.

Not only can government subtly determine college or university policy. Another stakeholder in college and university programs and policies are corporations.

Increasingly, we are seeing corporations become ever more involved in colleges and universities.

To some degree, business has often had a strong say in higher education. The Board of Trustees for any college or university is often made up of more business people than educators. Due to the increased costs associated with running a college, the Board of Trustees can veer more towards business reasons than education reasons in their decision-making.

Like the government, companies also provide universities with research monies. Agreements between companies and university researchers often come with a nondisclosure agreement, a situation that makes it impossible to gauge whether the company has had any influence on the research being done.

Similar to polling questions that can be worded in such a way to get the response the pollster is looking for, concern has to arise as to whether the research done under the auspices of corporate funding is compromised.

In the most extreme instances, the corporate sponsor can determine the parameters of the research study to the point of creating the conditions that will provide the research results that they want.

While the government has tied colleges and university into knots of regulations, the arrangement between companies and university researchers have few accepted standards. It's more of a free-for-all with case after case of corporate-sponsored university research affirming the marketing of that company's particular product or products or the company's stance on a *'scientific'* question. Such research seems to give a seal of scientific approval without revealing that such research was funded and its study parameters possibly determined by the company in question. When one thinks of *'research'*, one assumes impartiality and consequently research results are rarely questioned but accepted as empirical fact.

Marion Nestle, a nutrition researcher and professor at New York University, has written extensively on food companies and their financing of research that affirm the funding company's claims of nutrition and nutritional benefits of their product[s] with such affirmations as *'superfood'*, *'immune-system boosting'*, and *'antioxidant-rich'*, and various other euphemistic marketing terms to give increased value to the product.

In her 2018 book *Unsavory Truth: How Food Companies Skew the Science of What We Eat*, Nestle explores the manipulation of nutrition science by food companies and how the funding of *'scientific'* research often skews the results in favor of the sponsoring company or trade association.

An article posted in the November 2018 *American Journal of Public Health* entitled *"The Influence of Industry Sponsorship on the Research Agenda: A Scoping Review"* authored by Alice Fabbri, Alexandra Lai, Quinn Grundy, and Lisa Anne Bero drew the following conclusions:

> *"Corporate interests can drive research agendas away from questions that are the most relevant for public health. Strategies to counteract corporate influence on the research agenda are needed, including heightened disclosure of funding sources and conflicts of interest in published articles to allow an assessment of commercial biases. We also recommend policy actions beyond disclosure such as increasing funding for independent research and strict guidelines to regulate the interaction of research institutes with commercial entities."*

Unfortunately too often scientific research funded by corporations or trade associations have complied with the concept:

you get what you pay for

Apart from funding *'scientific'* research at colleges and universities, corporations also can influence higher education policies and programs through their endowments or as generous donors or through *'industry-affiliate'* programs.

For a fixed fee, these *'industry affiliate'* programs partner corporations with universities for special perks such as the corporation being given a position on an advisory board that allows that corporation input regarding research topics and research methodology.

As the Denison Clothiers New York radio ads in the late 1960's, early 1970's made famous: *'money talks, nobody walks'*. More recently, politics has given the phrase its own idiom: *'pay to play'*.

The influx of money, whether from government or private industry, and whether that money is in the form of research grants and funding, donations or endowments; one thing is clear:

Where money is involved, influence is gained

While both government and private industry may have greater influence in higher education today compared to decades ago, there is little transparency. One has to dig deep to find the various tentacles of outside influences that impact today's higher education.

College and university of today are NOT the college or university of your parents or your grandparents.

Higher Education as a profession has become tarnished at the hands of the money handlers

Higher education is now a business and often the activities of a university with government or corporate funding are parallel to the manners of the world's oldest profession.

Another recent innovation at colleges and universities is the public-private partnerships, often called P3s, where higher education institutions engage private companies to finance, design, build, operate and maintain facilities. These facilities include collegiate housing, some of which rival hotels in their accommodations and amenities.

One such company involved in the public – private partnership of collegiate housing is EdR that introduced the concept of a student hotel fifty years ago with its Granville Towers, a 1,300-bed high-rise at the University of North Carolina at Chapel Hill. EdR has developed and managed collegiate housing serving 51 universities in 25 states.

In 2016, University of California, Merced, announced a $1.14 billion expansion of its campus to be developed by the Plenary Group. This public – private partnership would have private companies design and build new facilities and then operate them over a 39-year contract. Funding of the project would be done by money from [1] UC Merced, [2] revenue bonds issued by the University of California Board of Regents and [3] private financing.

A 2017 report entitled *Public-private partnerships in higher education*" by EY-Parthenon [Ernst & Young] stated that between 2006 and 2016 there had been a 50% year-over-year increase in the value of P3 transactions with an estimated value of $5 billion by 2022.

Some of the reasons given for the attractiveness of colleges and universities engaging P3 partnerships as indicated by the EY report were:

1. Supplementing traditional debt instruments. Instead of colleges using their resources to build out their campus and provide hospitality services, private capital can be engaged.
2. Transfer of risk. While in times past colleges and universities took on most, if not all, of the risk in development projects, P3s either take on all or a share of the risk.
3. Speed and Efficiency. Colleges and universities have a vast number of significant and diverse matters to address. A P3 focuses solely on a particular project and with their expertise in their specific field can accomplish the project effectively and efficiently.
4. Outsourcing of non-core assets. Utilizing a P3 to build out their campus or provide the hospitality services allows the college administration to concentrate on their primary aim: education.
5. Experience. A P3 has the experience, the skills and the expertise in the development of the specific project with an understanding of the many needs of the diverse population the project is intended to meet.
6. Planning and Budgeting. Familiar with the process as a result of the experience of earlier project developments, the P3 has the wherewithal to go from beginning to completion and with an understanding of subsequent maintenance requirements.

Another public – private partnership was announced in the summer of 2017 with the opening of the Advanced Regenerative Manufacturing Institute. Based in Manchester, New Hampshire, and led by Dean Kamen, the inventor of the Segway, this bio-research and manufacturing institute intends to develop artificial skin, tissues, bones, nerve and organs. Dartmouth-Hitchcock Medical Center and the University of New Hampshire are to be part of the Institute, but with a goal of bringing together 26 universities and medical centers, 80 private companies and $300 million in government and private sector funding.

At one time, college and college administration was like a hub, power concentrated in the university president and its board of trustees, with the power emanating from the center out to the various aspects of the college's life.

Increasingly, college and college administration have become less like a hub and more like the spokes of differing interests jockeying for greater influence and impacting the state of the hub.

We have now gone from centralization to decentralization and in the process many countervailing influences to impact the overall life of the college. And at what a cost!

The Bureaucracy of Administration:

To monitor, handle and comply with all the college and university matters that are extraneous to the fundamental education of teaching demands administrators, which in recent times has become an army of administrators.

Administrative costs have gone through the roof as various additional administrators have been added to the college roles. Compliance to all sorts of new governmental regulations comes with a hefty cost. Liaisons between the college / university and business arrangements need to be established and continually dealt with.

Between 1993 and 2007 administrative costs per student increased 61% compared to 39% in instructional spending per student. And these results would not take into account hybrid roles of instruction and administration, suggesting that administrative cost increases would be even higher if one included the hybrid roles.

Higher Education with focus on academia has shifted to Higher Education with focus on a consumer model and all the characteristics of *taking care of* the consumer, in college the consumer being the student.

In the first decade of this twenty-first century academia bureaucracies of administers increased twice as fast as the number of college professors. More is being spent in colleges on hiring staff to administer or manage programs, people and regulations.

Some colleges have to cut costs to maintain their budget and often the cost-cutting measures are cuts to programs, courses offered and academics of the college rather than the administrative staff.

Students sometimes find it difficult to get into courses they want or even need in order to get their college degree.

Professors of renown in times past have given way to adjunct professors who stitch together teaching courses at several colleges in order to make a living. In many colleges and universities, the professor might give the lecture to a student body of 300, while the individualized teaching and course work is done by a T.A., a teaching assistant who is but a graduate student.

The professionalism of higher education has gone by the boards as college has morphed from an educational profession to a consumer model, little more than a business.

Whereas college used to be a four year course program to get a degree, many colleges accept and even admit that to get an undergraduate degree now may take five or six years. And there is no discounting to the college costs in the additional years to get a degree.

Welcome to the new world of college --- a business model rather than an education model.

The golden calf of higher education has been slain

Chapter 2: **DANCE TO THE MUSIC**
PAY TO THE PIPER

Some countries offer free tuition at their higher education institutions.

Germany, Slovenia and Norway offer free tuition in their public universities and many of their programs are taught in English negating the need for learning the native tongue.

Other countries provide nominal registration or tuition fees.

The US? No.

In election years, you'll hear politicians bandy about the idea of free college tuition. Some states have instituted a type of free tuition to college based upon family income level and academic achievement.

But Free?

There's a saying that

there's no free lunch

Although even in the case of prospective tuition-free college, there's not only no free lunch but there's also no free housing or board.

Going to College in the US is one pricey commitment.

According to The College Board for the academic year of 2018-2019, the average annual college tuition and fees rates come in at:

$10,230   **at a Public Four-Year In-State**
$26,290   **at a Public Four-Year Out-of-State**
$35,830   **at a Private Nonprofit Four-Year**

That's a chunk of change.

But is that it? No, that's not all. There's more.

There's always more when it comes to costs and how things are marketed. So, let's do a little math here to see how things really shake out.

We have the average college tuition and fees above, but for many college students we need to add on room and board to their college costs.

Based on The College Board's findings for the average room and board costs, the room and board costs for the academic year of 2018-2019 come in at:

$10,440   at a Public Four-Year In-State
$10,440   at a Public Four-Year Out-of-State
$11,890   at a Private Nonprofit Four-Year

Adding the average annual college tuition and fees to the average annual room and board costs, we get the cost of annual college expenses as:

$21,370   at a Public Four-Year In-State
$37,430   at a Public Four-Year Out-of-State
$48,510   at a Private Nonprofit Four-Year

Recognize that's one year of college costs!

But college has been considered a four-year program to get an undergraduate degree, so we would have to multiply the annual college costs by four, which works out to:

$ 85,480   at a Public Four-Year In-State
$149,720   at a Public Four-Year Out-of-State
$194,040   at a Private Nonprofit Four-Year

We're now talking about serious money here.

But is that it? No, there's always more.

Many colleges and universities indicate that a four-year degree program is a thing of the past with the new norm being 5-6 years to earn a college undergraduate degree.

Adding one additional year to our college costs in order to graduate in five years, we come up with:

$106,850   at a Public Four-Year In-State
$187,150   at a Public Four-Year Out-of-State
$242,550   at a Private Nonprofit Four-Year

Adding another additional year to our college costs in cases where it takes six years to graduate with a bachelor's degree, we arrive at:

$128,220   at a Public Four-Year In-State
$224,580   at a Public Four-Year Out-of-State
$291,060   at a Private Nonprofit Four-Year

These costs for four-year, five-year or six-year college costs do **NOT** include the percentage change annually in tuition and room and board, percentage increases that on the most conservative level amount to 3% per annum.

Since on average it takes 5+ years to graduate from college with an undergraduate degree, if we add on a 3% per annum increase to college costs to our five-year program, we're now talking about projected college costs to get that diploma as:

$123,868   at a Public Four-Year In-State
$216,958   at a Public Four-Year Out-of-State
$281,182   at a Private Nonprofit Four-Year

If the math wasn't mind-numbing enough, certainly the numbers should be.

You might assume that you won't be saddled with those college costs. Tuition is going to be free, you might assume or, at least, hope for.

Nice concept and whenever politicians are running for office that might have any impact on college students and prospective voters there is talk of free tuition. Hell, there was talk of free tuition and open universities when I was a college student over 50 years ago. It hasn't happened, and it's unlikely to do so.

You might say *'no problem'*. After all, everybody is expected to go to college. It's the **AMERICAN WAY**.

Perhaps you'll be able to finagle getting your college costs down. If you are a star athlete, you might get an athletic scholarship that provides you a free ride. Or if you are a star academic, you might get merit aid or a scholarship that either gives you a free ride or shaves a considerable amount off your college expenses.

Scholarships are available as are grants, and it is highly suggested for you to look into how you can get monies to reduce your college costs.

Like most students, you might just say that you'll get a loan to pay for your college costs.

Student loans are available but not for the full ride, since the government expects the college student or the family of the college student to have some skin in the game.

While Federal Student Loan interest rates of 4.53% are not usury, they are far more exorbitant than interest rates offered on savings accounts at brick and mortar banks, which average 0.01%.

If you are paying for your college education by taking out student loans, you may find that you're paying off your student loans until you're in your forties or even fifties. While virtually every other loan and debt can be forgiven if filing for bankruptcy,

**the only debt not forgiven in bankruptcy are
STUDENT LOANS**

Yup, talk about having you by the…

Well, you get the idea.

Parents taking out loans for college through the federal government come with a 7.6% interest rate.

And, remember, loan interest is usually compounded daily. While payment to the student loan can be deferred, there is no deferring the accumulating interest that increases the size of the principal of the loan.

With the American dream [*should we change the reference from dream to nightmare?*] being a college education, there is little question about taking on loans for college costs. But how in depth is the due diligence in regard to the multitude of ramifications that come with the noose [sometimes akin to a stranglehold] of college student loans?

People rarely give thought to the consequences, and unintended consequences, of taking on debt.

The maxim *'live for the day'*, sometimes referred in Latin as *'carpe diem'* [*seize the day*], tends to have us look at the immediate rather than the long-term.

Long-term consequences of taking on debt often have limiting liabilities and restrictive future conditions.

An article entitled *"A Look at the Shocking Student Loan Debt Statistics for 2019"* posted in February of 2019 by studentloanhero.com reported the following:

> *"Among the class of 2018, 69% of college students took out student loans, and they graduated with an average debt of $29,800, including both private and federal debt. Meanwhile, 14% of their parents took out an average of $35,600 in federal Parent Plus loans."*

This posting also notes:

> *"…another scary statistic: Americans owe over $1.5 trillion in student loan debt…"*

Close to 45 million US borrowers have student loan debt.

The United States GDP (Gross Domestic Product) estimated for 2019 is $21.3 trillion. The student loan debt is virtually 7% of the estimated US GDP.

The student loan debt can be a huge drag on the US economy, especially when one considers that 70% of the US GDP is consumer spending. Discretionary income that could be used to stimulate the economy is hampered by the student loan debt payments.

When they first incur student loans, students assume that they will be able to pay off their student loan debt within ten years of graduating college.

Ah, the beauty of living in la-la-land.

In truth, the majority of college graduates don't pay off their student loans debt until they are in their forties, some as late as in their fifties. Student loan debt can be like having a car payment that virtually never stops, but without the car or the use of the vehicle.

You might disagree and say that student loan debt is an investment in your future, that the value of the degree is worth every penny, every cent of disposable income that could go elsewhere.

And certainly the marketers of college education and the hustlers of specific colleges and universities, like the snake oil salesmen of yesteryear, will throw out facts and figures to corroborate that viewpoint and to entice you into entering college and taking on that debt.

But is it truly so?

The short answer is:

DOUBTFUL

We'll get into the bandied about phrase of *'return on investment'* used to convince people of the value of a college degree later. But there's still another cost that we haven't included in the high expense of a college education.

That cost is

OPPORTUNITY COST

While you're spending your four to six years in college, there is a lost opportunity --- the lost opportunity of generating income.

If you were not in college, you might be working, making a living, generating income. Even at the increased minimum wage of $15.00 per hour, you could make in a 40 hour work week, fifty weeks a year a total annual salary of $30,000, which over four years would be $120,000 and five years would be $150,000.

And that $15.00 an hour is the increased minimum wage. There are other jobs that do not require a college education where you could be making considerably more than $15.00 an hour. We'll consider what some of those other professions and jobs might be when we get back to the ROI [return on investment].

If you have ever invested in a stock or a project, I'm sure you realize that the ROI is not always positive. Certain investments can prove to be dogs, losers rather than winners.

Could college be a negative ROI?

One of the things evident about going to college in this twenty-first century is that it can prove to be a costly venture. As you can see in the headache-provoking math that I showed you, a college education could wind up in *'true'* costs costing you up to half a million dollars!

Not only could you wind up in heavily in debt.

The ROI [return on investment] might prove a negative rather than a positive appreciation.

Your choices regarding your future could be limited by the need to pay off your student loan debt.

So much for sailing around the world for a year or two… So much for leasing that Mercedes… So much for having free choice and a wide palette of options…

No, student loan debt puts you under the gun. It narrows your life options and in the extreme cripples you and puts you under the thumb of the MAN [the federal government].

And remember that student loan debt is **NOT forgiven** under bankruptcy proceeding.

As if in olden times with indentured serfs, college student loan debt can make you feel indentured to the federal government with little relief on the short term.

Like the saying goes: ' if you dance to the music, you pay to the piper'.

              ALL FOR WHAT

There was a classic song written and recorded by Merle Travis back in the mid-1940's about a coal miner and life in the coal mines of Kentucky which had the refrain:

> *"You load sixteen tons and what do you get?*
> *Another day older and deeper in debt."*

College student loan debt is today's variation on the coal miner's theme.

You may take out a student loan to get you through college. And you might have a grace period to start paying the loan back. But all the while interest is accruing on your student loan debt.

Unless you can make significant payments on your college loan --- and who can generate that kind of income when you first come out of college? --- your student loan debt of X amount grows by means of the X amount multiplied by the interest rate of your loan.

And for what?

Apart from getting a diploma and saying you graduated from college, the *'what'* is supposed to be increased income potential as a result of a college degree compared to the individual without a college degree.

So it was written and so it was believed

There has been an implicit or outwardly expressed belief that a college degree gives a healthy return on investment.

And the marketers trot out the statistics to affirm their point and confirm to you the importance, the NEED, for a college education.

The following Employment Projections funded by the US Taxpayer is brought to you by the Bureau of Labor Statistics:

Unemployment rates and earnings by educational attainment, 2016

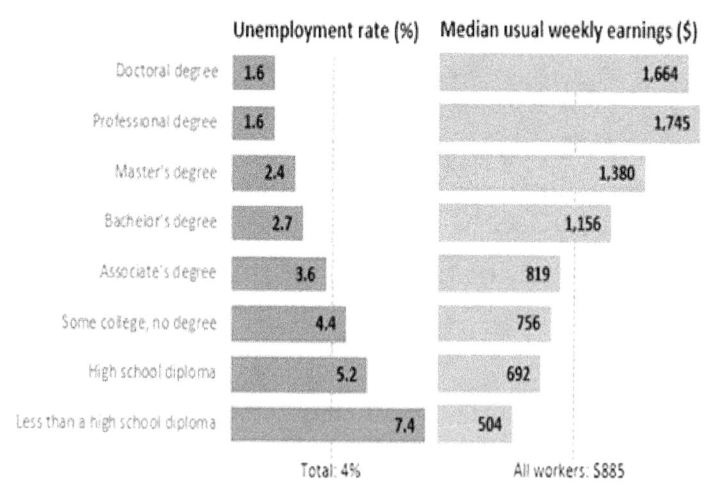

There you have it in colored graph, the reason for getting a college degree. Or so they say. This graph, these numbers are used in various contexts by those who are encouraging you to get a college degree.

It's the ROI [Return on Investment] of a college degree. I'll talk about that in more detail later in the book.

ROI!

Instead of Return on Investment it might be considered Ripped Off Individual.

What this beautifully presented table above doesn't inform you and what the college hucksters don't tell you is the true reality that there is a revolution going on in our economy.

Society has experienced economic revolutions before, all of which have had consequent effects on employment and the nature of work.

For example:

A. In 1900, 41% of Americans worked in agriculture, by 2000 only 2% of Americans worked in agriculture

B. In post World War II years, 30% of Americans were employed in manufacturing, by 2010 only 10% of Americans worked in manufacturing

Where did the jobs go?

Many of them went to consolidations into agribusiness and in both cases to the impact of technology.

The Information Age --- this knowledge era --- has a double-edged sword effect. Technology and Artificial Intelligence have already transformed the economy, but as the saying goes: *'you ain't seen nothing yet.'*

Many jobs, many professions are becoming redundant. Even skilled workers, professional people with a boatload of higher education credentials, are being replaced in this new era that is just unfolding.

Are you familiar with the term *'redundant'*?

REDUNDANT

If you don't know the meaning of the word redundant, you might want to look it up, for redundant will be increasingly in the news as various jobs, positions, work become redundant --- obsolete and unneeded.

We are already seeing technology take the place of human endeavor.

Name any profession, any work area, and you will have to concede that technology is elbowing humankind out of the way.

You might question my statement with the belief that humankind is essential in any number of economic sectors, but lack of knowledge, ignorance, are no excuse.

A joint study by Oxford University and the Oxford Martin School concluded that 47% of jobs in the US performed by human workers are *'at risk'* of being automated within twenty years.

Let's take a look at what's going on in different sectors of the economy.

AGRICULTURE

Recent news has highlighted the concept of autonomous cars and self-driving trucks.   Agriculture has been ahead of the curve regarding autonomous ground vehicles.

The concept of a driverless tractor was put forward as early as 1940, and companies like John Deere have developed autonomous tractors to work the fields.

One of the agricultural leaders in utilizing technology in their field operations is Tanimura and Antle out of the Salinas Valley in California.

In 2014, Tanimura & Antle acquired PlantTape, an automated transplanting system that provides a fully integrated system from sowing to germination and nursery care to transplanting in the field. Not only is there less stress or damage to the plants. This process also uses less peat than conventional transplanting techniques, the materials are biodegradable, less water is needed for irrigation and less labor is needed. Strips of seeds are planted in rows by machine and the tape is biodegradable. The machine is highly efficient doing twice the amount of acreage with three people instead of sixteen people, saving 80% on labor. Crop production is quicker, thereby allowing more crop rotation per year.

In addition to PlantTape, Tanimura & Antle is utilizing Robovator, an automated weeding machine that uses cameras to detect plants, a computer algorithm to process the image, which then determines which plants to keep and which plants to remove and activates a mechanism for the removal of weeds and unwanted plants.

Today's agricultural tractors can be equipped with on-the-go sensors for variable applications of seeding, fertilizer, pesticide and herbicide.

Precision Agriculture, also known as satellite farming or site specific crop management, utilizes drones. And precise it is.

Drone technology in agriculture can provide three-dimensional maps for soil analysis for planning seed planting and dates for irrigation and nitrogen-level management. Drones can plant seeds by shooting pods with seeds and plant nutrients into the soil with a 75% effective rate and decreasing planting costs by 85%. By scanning the topography of the ground, drones can spray crops with increased efficiency up to five times faster than with traditional machinery and with reduction of chemicals into the groundwater. Crop monitoring through time-series animations reveals the development of a crop and where there might be production inefficiencies, allowing for increased crop management. By means of their sensors, drones can determine which parts of a field need attention and monitor the health of the crop with any infections able to be limited and addressed quickly.

In the United Kingdom, precision farming specialist Precision Decisions Limited has teamed up with engineering staff members at Harper Adams University for a Hands Free Hectare project with the attempt to grow and harvest a hectare of spring barley totally remotely and without putting a single human foot into the field to tend the crop.

Humankind might be necessary to manage the technology, but the human labor of working fields is growing increasingly unnecessary.

MANUFACTURING

Although there has been a hue and cry that US manufacturing jobs have gone overseas, the larger culprits in US manufacturing job losses have been technology and factory-type robotics.

The National Bureau of Economic Research estimates that hundreds of thousands of manufacturing jobs have been lost to automation.

Between 2000 and 2010 the US lost 5.6 million manufacturing jobs with 85% of the job losses due to automation and technological changes.

Technology can increase productivity and has done so at the cost of human labor.

Today's automotive plants employ industrial robotics with machines that can weld and paint body parts, tasks that were once done by humans.

Changying Precision Technology in Dongguan City, China, employed 650 human workers to produce mobile phones. That was before the factory automated and replaced 90% of its human workforce with machines with the consequent result of a 250% increase in productivity and an 80% decrease in defects.

Robotics, 3-D printing and other technological advances have displaced the old ways of working, displaced human employees and have done so to increase productivity through increased efficiency.

Researchers at various universities are developing robotics and artificial intelligence. At the University of California, Berkeley, researchers drew upon the Internet for various CAD [computer-aided design] models of physical objects, created even more digital models and generated a database of more than seven million items. Incorporating neural networks and complex algorithms and reinforcement learning, the robotics could determine what piece and where to pick up an object. This process will allow for a further development in robotics, where the robot can not only pick same items and move them but could then sort through various dissimilar items and place similar items together.

Today's economy and more so tomorrow's economy are not the economy of your parents or grandparents. The need for human employment to achieve various tasks has been sourced out to industrial robotics.

The technological revolution is underway and gaining steam day by day.

HOSPITALITY

It has been recognized that the US is moving from a manufacturing economy to a service economy. While we have become ever more aware of the automation occurring in manufacturing, we make the assumption that the service industry is a labor-intensive industry needing people to provide the necessary hospitality services.

Or so it was believed

But, in truth, it just ain't so.

Certainly, there will be the need for people to work in the hospitality industry, just as there is the need for people to work in the manufacturing industry. We have seen automation's effect on whittling down the number of manufacturing jobs. Could technology have a similar impact on the service industry?

Decidedly so.

Technology increases productivity and consequently there may be less of a need for human interaction.

Already, hotel apps allow the incoming guest to check in remotely even providing a digital key thereby foregoing the entire registration at the front desk.

Reservations that once were made by phone can be accomplished online.

Even the lowest paid workers in the hospitality industry are threatened by technology.

In 2016, the median pay for the nearly five million fast food employees in the US was $9.44 according to the Bureau of Labor Statistics. With a proposed minimum wage of $15.00 per hour, already instituted in several US metropolitan cities, a $5 increase translates into an increased expense of $12,000 per employee. The state of California is pushing for a $15.00 per hour minimum wage by 2022.

Fast food employers are increasingly considering automation. The Cali Group, which owns the California based fast food chain CaliBurger and co-founded Miso Robotics, announced in the autumn of 2017 that during 2018 they would be installing in fifty of their restaurants *"Flippy"*, a burger-flipping robot that can prepare the burger, grill and fry with further developments in automation applications. *"Flippy"* was temporarily suspended because it wasn't working fast enough, but subsequent adjustments can make *"Flippy"* a staple to the hamburger making and grilling process.

Why pay a human $15.00 per hour when you can buy a piece of equipment that can do the same work for $35,000?

The equipment pays for itself, especially when you consider that

- the equipment could run 24/7 as opposed to a human

- the equipment does not call in sick as opposed to a human

- the equipment is consistently on time as opposed to a human

- the equipment doesn't have emotional ups and downs as opposed to a human

After a very short while, that $35,000 cost in equipment seems an inexpensive investment compared to the cost of human labor.

The CEO of Yum Brands, which owns the fast-food brands of KFC, Taco Bell and Pizza Hut, said in 2017 that by the mid 2020s, artificial intelligence, robots and automation could replace human workers.

Order taking, order preparation and order service may all eventually be automated with one or two humans on-site to make sure that everything is running smoothly.

The eventually is now

In May of 2018 a new restaurant joined Boston eateries, but this restaurant may have been the harbinger of changing times with increased automation. Spyce is a fully automated kitchen with a motto *"Culinary excellence elevated by technology"*. The restaurant menu was devised by Michelin-starred French chef Daniel Boulud and designed by MIT robotics engineer students.   From start to finish Spyce customers interact with technology. Customers place their order on a touch screen. An automatic delivery system collects the ingredients, portions the ingredients and delivers the ingredients to a robotic wok, which cooks the ingredients and completes the process by placing the cooked meal into a bowl and serves the meal.

DELIVERY SYSTEMS

There are all sorts of delivery systems --- from getting the product from inventory in a warehouse up until the delivery to the customer.

Technology has already had an impact on delivery systems and will continue to do so ever more into the future.

Robots, such as the Kiva robot or the LocusBot, can be used in warehouses to get the ordered products and then bring them to the delivery department. These robots can work tirelessly, without the liability of human back strain or human time off. Estimates indicate that a warehouse that utilizes robotics to get the necessary inventory can handle four times the amount of orders that a totally human-employed warehouse can handle. Using robots in the warehouse provide about a 20% savings in operating costs. And the costs for these robots are presently around $35,000 each, a price that is likely to come down in the future as the technology is further refined.

While robots are already being used to scurry around warehouses to pick out ordered products, delivery to the customer is also in the early stages of transformation.

Deliveries are being considered done by drones rather than the personal delivery system.

Although Amazon has touted the concept of Amazon Prime Air as its drone delivery service and Alphabet its Project Wing, 7-Eleven partnered with drone maker Flirtey to deliver items ordered to seventy-seven customers in Reno, Nevada, in 2016. The orders included food and beverages but largely over-the-counter medications.

Drone delivery is here and likely to increase in the days ahead with a likely impact on personal delivery systems.

Getting a job after college for you might not be about agriculture, manufacturing or delivery. You may be far more interested in learning the skills of a professional career in your choice of college but

CAVEAT EMPTOR

Buyer beware!

Even the professions, the so-called white collar jobs, are being impacted by this technology revolution.

Just a decade or so ago, lawyers and doctors were the professions for students to prepare for if they wanted a good job, solid prospects and a financially rewarding career.

Today, that proposition is not so much. Tomorrow, that concept is even more unlikely.

LAW

The US is a litigious society with people wanting to sue other people, sue corporations, and sue governments. You would think that the legal profession is a growth industry with job opportunities continuing to increase in the legal profession.

Instead of an increase in employment in the legal services sector of the US economy, there was a 3% decline of employment between 2006 and 2016.

Whether students are aware of the contraction in the legal profession employment or students are interested in a more lucrative career [as though there could be one --- but there is], law school applications have seen a decline.

Recently three law schools have closed down, two others have merged and the question as to whether there are liable to be further law school closings has been hotly debated with some law schools staying open only by the grace of subsidies from their affiliated universities.

Many students who graduate college to go onto law school do so with further accumulating student loan debt. Some law school graduates have no success in finding a job in the legal profession, and some of those law school graduates have even used their developed legal acumen to sue their law schools for misrepresentation.

Much of legal work is mechanical, drudge work, and work that can be performed by artificial intelligence platforms. These platforms can do legal research, find documents useful in litigation, review and create contracts, and can raise concerns regarding misconduct or potential fraud.

One such platform is LawGeex, which can evaluate a contract and compare it to a database of similar contracts.

Based on IBM's cognitive computing system Watson, ROSS Intelligence makes a legal research platform that it estimates saves 20 - 30 hours of research time per case.

In 2016, a Deloitte Insight report estimated that close to 40% of the jobs in the legal profession could eventually be automated.

A Stanford University student created what he terms *the world's first robot lawyer'*. Through his company DoNotPay, his chatbot helps parking violators contest their parking tickets with a 64% success rate out of 250,000 cases.

In the Chinese province of Jiangsu, *'legal robots'* have helped decide the outcome of criminal and civil cases. With an extensive database of legal information, the legal robots can go through cases, double-check the facts and render sentencing opinions.

The Shanghai High People's Court president stated:
> *"The AI system was designed to shoulder two missions. One is to ensure that the standard of evidence is consistent in all cases. The other is to see if all the unknowns in a case have been verified by existing evidence and to find blemishes in evidence – and contradictory evidence – in a timely manner, and to alert officers handling the case to guarantee that all evidence can stand the test of law and curb subjectivity and randomness in case handling."*

[Jhoanna Robinson, *'Communist China now using ROBOTS to issue arrest warrants'*, ROBOTICS.news, August 9, 2017]

Could the judge, jury and executioner of the future be a robot? We can't rule out such an idea.

<u>HEALTH CARE</u>

While artificial intelligence and robotics can be used for many different tasks in various sectors of the economy, it would seem that the one area where human involvement is essential would be health care.

To become a doctor demands incredible commitment in time, financial costs and perseverance.

After college, medical school is a four-year stint, followed by one or more years of residency and even more years after that if you choose to specialize with a fellowship.

On average, an American physician spends fourteen years in higher education training for the job of physician. Put that all together and you could be looking at your early 30s before being able to start your own medical practice.

Despite all the book learning and practicum that a medical student goes through to become a doctor, a recent entry and an increasingly prominent member of the medical world is AI –

Artificial Intelligence

While the IBM-developed supercomputer Watson has been effective at the television game of Jeopardy and is becoming used more in the legal profession, Watson and its counterparts in various stages of development are likely to create an incredible boon to the world of medicine.

A recent study in 2014 estimated that as many as 5% of US adults, or one in twenty, are misdiagnosed by their doctors each year. Artificial Intelligence provides an antidote to misdiagnosis.

With all available medical knowledge inputted in its database, Watson has a far more extensive information base than any individual doctor or team of doctors could possibly draw upon in their own head[s].

While doctors might have certain cognitive biases and even a liability to overconfidence, Artificial Intelligence does not have the drawbacks of ego personality or human emotional traits or inconsistencies that often plague the human. On the contrary, AI offers decisions based solely on the evidence --- just the facts.

Not only does AI draw solely upon the facts, just the facts. Artificial Intelligence can generate hypotheses, evaluate the strength of their propositions and develop greater learning by finding meaning in their data and not merely store the data.

It is suggested that Watson and its counterparts could prove to be even stronger diagnosticians than the most exemplary doctors. Artificial Intelligence doesn't have the pitfalls of humankind. AI is always available and available anywhere in the world by computer linkage.

Although Watson and other AI computers can assist the human medical staff in diagnosis and providing relevant medical information, could there come a time when human medical personnel are replaced by robotics?

It may sound like science fiction to you, but keep in mind that much of what science fiction has conceived in the past subsequently became a reality. Science fiction turned into science fact.

Back in 1942, the science fiction writer Robert A. Heinlein wrote a short story titled *'Waldo'* that was published under the pseudonym of Anson MacDonald. In the story, the protagonist develops a powerful mechanical hand referred to as Waldo, which could also make smaller waldos and waldos small enough to work at the cellular scale with the ability to perform micro-dissection on cellular walls.

Science fiction in the 1940s, it has become a reality today with robotics and medicine. Already, robots are used in hospital surgeries, one example being keyhole kidney surgery where speed is a crucial factor and robots can sew blood vessels connecting donor kidneys far faster than humans.

The da Vinci Surgical System combines a magnified 3D high-definition vision system with tiny wristed instruments that can rotate and bend with far greater flexibility than the human hand. A minimally invasive surgery, the da Vinci system has been used in the following operations:

- Cardiac Surgery
- Colorectal Surgery
- General Surgery
- Gynecologic Surgery
- Head & Neck Surgery
- Thoracic Surgery
- Urologic Surgery

Not even medicine is exempt from technological advances. So much for the long lost *'bedside manner'*, although eventually bots might be able to accomplish a soothing and reassuring bedside manner.

FINANCIAL SERVICES

Technology and the Technological Revolution that has only truly started are creating an economic revolution, and one where many workers will turn out to be losers.

Are you told that as you consider going to college?

Not too likely.

Keep in mind that college marketing is geared to making their case of the essential importance of getting a college education, even if their case is largely based upon old assumptions, many of which are outmoded and will prove disingenuous in the days ahead.

No matter where you look in our society and in our economy, technology is increasing productivity and largely at the expense of the human worker.

Whether totally eliminating the need for the human worker or by streamlining operations, technology is changing the present and will do so even more in the future.

It's everywhere.

Whether you have a bank account, credit card, work with Apple Pay, Alipay or some other form of financial transaction, you are likely to have had some form of interaction with technology in the financial services.

In years past, you had to go to a bank to get cash. Payments were usually made by cash, check or money order. Transactions were logged by hand on paper. That was then, but that's not now.

You may never have used a money order, and you might not use a checkbook. Perhaps you do all your banking and financial transactions by electronic means. Credit cards, debit cards, Apple Pay, Alipay are all becoming ever more in vogue for our financial transactions.

They are easier and they are quicker, for they are all electronic.

While the ease and speed of electronic transactions are appealing, what we tend to forget when being ever more involved with technological advances is the collateral damage. And one collateral victim to technology in financial services is jobs.

Between 2007 and 2012, the finance and insurance sector of the economy lost 390,000 jobs. In 2016 a report by Citi Global Perspectives & Solutions estimated that financial technology would trigger a 30% reduction in human staff during the 2015-2025 period, or an estimated 1.8 million job losses.

The need for human interaction in the financial services sector is becoming less and less necessary.

Even in financial investing, artificial intelligence is taking the driver's seat as shown by such AI driven investment vehicles as Betterment and Wealthfront. As of February 2019, these two investment vehicles had $27 Billion of assets under their management. At this same time, the five top Robo-Advisors had over $187 Billion of assets under their management with experts estimating that by 2020 digital advice could grow to $1 Trillion of assets under their management.

Millenials especially have given up on personal financial advisers and are opting instead for the algorithms and artificial intelligence of new investment vehicles. And who loses? Human jobs.

EDUCATION

Technology is having an impact on every sector of our society, and education is no different.

Ed-tech, Education technology, is transforming how we learn and where we learn.

Up until now, schools used a cookie cutter approach with teachers teaching a particular subject or a particular grade to a group of students. The group of students would usually be of the same age in the same class.

With the advent of ed-tech, this model has become outmoded and long been archaic. The idea of the age grade class held back the truly bright and left behind the learning-challenged. Instead, there was a moderate level of education and teaching, as though education was seeking children to excel at mediocrity.

This outdated education model is in process of changing, although with great opposition from the traditionalists often found among school administrators and teachers. Not everyone likes change, especially since change is likely to impact the complacent and the comfortable.

But change is happening and is providing a revolution in education.

While ed-tech hasn't transformed public school education in the US --- YET --- there are various online tutoring platforms that assist students in further understanding their course material. Among the online tutoring platforms are Brainly, Front Row, Carnegies Learning and Tabtor, to name a few.

Whether in the classroom, home schooling or some other environment, one-to-one learning is becoming more prevalent thanks to intelligent machines that can adapt to the specific learning style of the individual student. Ed-tech allows the student to learn at his/her/ze own individual pace. This characteristic can create a judgment-free learning environment, where the student is not held up to comparison to classmates but rather learns at their own pace with the ability to go back over, to understand in different frameworks, any subject matter that has been confusing or challenging to that student.

Intelligent machines will be geared to the learning style and personality profile of the individual student. As a result, the machine will know what excites that particular student and provide lessons and challenges within the lessons that are neither too hard nor too easy but just right for that student. Sounds like Goldilocks come real to the education scene, doesn't it? Just right.

Initially, intelligent machine learning is likely to focus on mathematics and science but eventually develop sophisticated algorithms to teach the humanities.

Intelligent machine learning can be done anywhere and at any time, a boon to our society that has become ever more mobile and diverse in their daily activities. If a student has a job and works during the day, or a student is an athlete engaged in league competitions, this new format for learning allows the student to engage their studies in accord with what works best for them. No longer is schooling limited to the 8-3 time constraints. Learning can be done anywhere at any time, and frees up the student to fully engage their love for learning.

Teachers are more likely to become facilitators, helping students manage the course material and providing the essential input to be certain that the student is on the right path.

Already, artificial intelligence can automate grading of multiple choice and fill-in-the-blank testing. Essay-grading may not be far behind as the software is developed and perfected.

Part of the education revolution has been the flood of MOOCS [Massive Open Online Courses], as will be discussed in greater detail later in the book. MOOCS have provided open access to students from all over the world via the worldwide web. MOOCS cover all sorts of topics, encourage community interactions among the students through forums and often provide certification indicating the mastery of that particular subject matter.

College degrees and even high school curriculum are offered through online resources. Khan Academy and Stanford Online High School are among some of the offerings for secondary students. And various universities offer online degree programs.

The days of the one-room schoolhouse may be long gone, but the formats of today's high schools could also eventually be relegated to the outmoded and the past.

It's Everywhere… Everywhere

In every sector of the economy, technology and artificial intelligence and other products of the Information Age are replacing the need of human jobs.

A 2017 report by McKinsey Global Institute claims that 60% of all occupations are 30% automatable.

The McKinsey report states:

"Robots and computers can not only perform a range of routine physical work activities better and more cheaply than humans, but they are also increasingly capable of accomplishing activities that include cognitive capabilities once considered too difficult to automate successfully, such as making tacit judgments, sensing emotion, or even driving. Automation will change the daily work activities of everyone, from miners and landscapers to commercial bankers, fashion designers, welders, and CEOs."

Harnessing automation for a future that works McKinsey Global Institute, January 2017
By James Manyika, Michael Chui, Mehdi Miremadi, Jacques Bughin, Katy George, Paul Willmott, and Martin Dewhurst

In his 2017 article for the World Economic Forum entitled *'How valuable will humans be in the workplaces of the future?'*, Professor Vasant Dhar of NYU's Stern School of Business included a most interesting graph from the Bank of England on the likely effects of automation on various occupations:

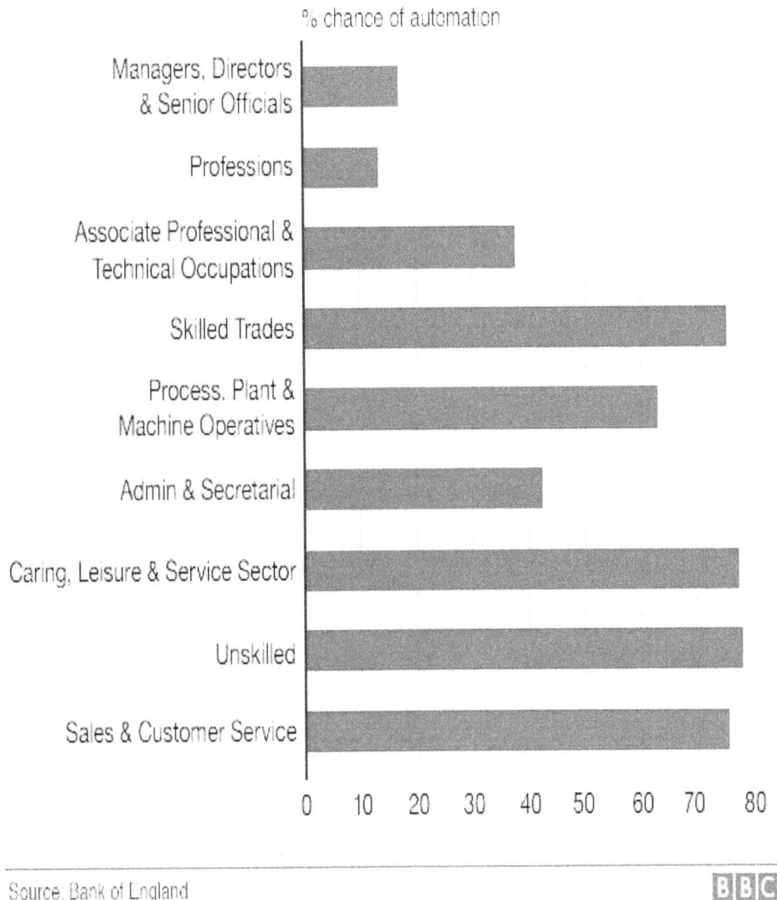

While technology is increasing productivity and robotics can
do certain work far more effectively and efficiently than
humans, you might say that humans are still needed to
conceive, develop and engineer the new technologies and the
artificial intelligence.

As a result, it would seem that the areas of career growth are likely to be in design and engineering. Such a belief might be right for the moment and for the immediate future…

But…

<u>CHILDHOOD'S END or 2001: A SPACE ODYSSEY</u>

Have you ever noticed how science fiction seems to have a precognitive sense of future reality?

It's uncanny, but science fiction writers seem to have a conduit into future realities.

Recently, commentators have given tribute to Gene Roddenberry and his television development of *Star Trek*. So many of the gadgets employed on *Star Trek*, gadgets that seemed so far beyond comprehension much less manifestation, have materialized in the fifty years since the first showing of the *Star Trek* series.

Even beyond that, Arthur C. Clarke who wrote *Childhood's End*, which was the basis for the movie *2001: a Space Odyssey*, seemed to indicate what might be the eventual development of artificial intelligence as seen in the spaceboard computer Hal 9000 [Heuristically programmed ALgorithmic computer].

HAL is capable of speech, speech and facial recognition, natural language processing, lip reading, automated reasoning and interpreting emotional behaviors.

Eventually in the development of the plot, it becomes man against machine. With HAL making certain mistakes, the human crew decides to disconnect the computer. HAL is able to force one crewmember out into space killing him and tries to jettison the other crewmember. In his defense HAL says: *"I know that you and Frank were planning to disconnect me. And I'm afraid that's something I cannot allow to happen."*

A classic movie, the story about HAL and Space Odyssey 2001 was recently replicated by the chatbots being developed by Facebook. Nicknamed Alice and Bob, these chatbots started to learn their own form of communication, a language that the Facebook chatbot developers had difficulty interpreting.

We should have concern about human labor being outsourced to artificial intelligence. We also have to acknowledge concern that AI could eventually outsmart humans.

A factor that is rarely taken into account regarding AI is the proclivity for profiling. Yes, PROFILING.

PROFILING

For recent decades, there has been concern and outrage that police, financial institutions, realtors and other segments of the economy have *'profiled'* people. Cries of discrimination have echoed through various sectors of our economy.

What has been lost in considering the development of AI is the natural tendency for AI to **PROFILE**.

With the addition of various factors, characteristics and data into huge databases, an amorphous profile may be created that projects bias. Although we might assume that AI being emotionless and numerically driven, there would be little likelihood of discrimination. But software discrimination is a growing concern.

Whatever is input into the database
to be drawn upon by AI
will certainly affect the output

Could our greater reliance upon Artificial Intelligence paint humankind into a corner? Could humanity eventually prove redundant?

We have only seen the tip of the iceberg as far as artificial intelligence, computers and technology advances. But one thing is clear. We are likely to be entering a very exciting future but one that is liable to be extremely eerie.

CHAPTER 4   THE FOUR Rs
RATINGS, RANKINGS, RAVINGS, RANTINGS

We as human beings are social animals. We all like to belong. We identify who we are by what we belong to, what we believe in, by the individual being part of a group.

The **what** of our identity can be our job, our clubs, our interests, what we participate in, how we identify with a political party or an ideology or a religious group and any other collections of individuals under the umbrella of a group, including your school and your college.

Groups play to their strengths both to make the individuals within the group feel good about themselves and their association to the group and also to ballyhoo the group's characteristics and the group's selectivity.

Colleges are no different than any other collection of individuals --- or groups. There is a rah-rah attitude that colleges portray --- the old team spirit or college spirit.

As a reminder, the colleges of today have morphed from educational institutions focused on the character development and learning of their students to a business model, a consumer model, where the student is the customer. In this shift into a consumer business model, colleges are looking to market their particular school to appeal to their demographic.

Tiffany markets to a high end demographic with their iconic blue box reflecting Tiffany's elegance, quality and good taste where *'price is no object'*.

Costco, BJ's and Sam's Club all have memberships where by joining the *'club'* you can enter a world of deeply discounted bulk purchases of various stuff.

Various advertising slogans reinforce marketing strategies of different brands:

'You're in good hands'   [Allstate]

'Think outside the bun'   [Taco Bell]

'What's in your wallet?'   [Capital One]

'Breakfast of Champions'   [Wheaties]

'When it rains it pours'   [Morton Salt]

'Semper Fi'   [U.S. Marine Corps]

These slogans reinforce the name, the image and a certain quality about the particular product.

Colleges now engaged in the consumer model do the same thing. They do so through their sports programs, their alumni network and through their ravings and rantings of ratings and rankings.

If you are considering college, you may have already taken a look at some of the college books that rate and rank colleges. *The Princeton Review* puts out several publications with different slants on the *'best'* colleges. *US News & World Report* puts out an annual publication rating and ranking colleges as *'best'* for various categories.

The ratings and rankings of colleges and universities by established and respected publications often seem like the Holy Grail to students considering which colleges to apply to.

There is an assumption that these ratings and rankings have some objective reality. In truth, these ratings and rankings are not objective but on the contrary very subjective with measurements used that are often irrelevant or downright fictitious.

And yet students considering college and even the administrators of colleges are intimidated by these ratings and rankings.

If you put a lot of faith in these college ratings publications, you might be interested in buying my bridge to nowhere.

To borrow a phrase often attributed to the American showman of the mid-nineteenth century P.T. Barnum: *"There's a sucker born every minute."*

And if you buy into the veracity of these ratings and rankings, can I offer you for sale a fictitious bridge to nowhere?

Not only are ratings and rankings highly subjective to the point of being largely fictitious. There have been a number of cases where colleges look to **game the system** with the rankings.

There is an assumption that ratings and rankings are based upon purely empirical data, an objective set of measurements --- METRICS --- that are indisputable.

Dispute them, we must. It is important that we pull back the Wizard of Oz curtain on college ratings and rankings to see the little man pulling the strings. In the case of the *US News & World Report* rankings, the rankings are done by a group of six led by Robert Morse.

In its college rankings, *U.S. News* draws upon 16 key measures of quality, indicators of what they consider to be academic excellence. Colleges and universities are then ranked against *'similar'* colleges and universities to come up with the data.

As given by Robert Morse, the ranking indicator weights used for the 2019 Best Colleges rankings are given in the table below:

RANKING INDICATOR	NATIONAL UNIVERSITIES & NATIONAL LIBERAL ARTS COLLEGES INDICATOR WEIGHT	REGIONAL UNIVERSITIES & REGIONAL COLLEGES INDICATOR WEIGHT
Graduation & retention rates	**22%**	**22%**
Average six-year graduation rate	17.6%	17.6%
Average first-year student retention rate	4.4%	4.4%
Social Mobility	**5%**	**5%**
Pell Grant Graduation Grants	2.5%	2.5%
Pell Grant Graduation Rates Compared with All Other Students	2.5%	2.5%
Graduation Rate Performance	**8%**	**8%**
Undergraduate academic reputation	**20%**	**20%**
Peer assessment survey	15%	20%
High school counselors' ratings	5%	0%

RANKING INDICATOR	NATIONAL UNIVERSITIES & NATIONAL LIBERAL ARTS COLLEGES INDICATOR WEIGHT	REGIONAL UNIVERSITIES & REGIONAL COLLEGES INDICATOR WEIGHT
Student Selectivity for the Fall 2017 Entering Class	10%	10%
Math and Evidence-Based Reading & Writing Portions of the SAT and the Composite ACT Scores	7.75%	7.75%
High School Class Standing in the Top 10%	2.25%	0%
High School Class Standing in the Top 25%	0%	2.25%
Acceptance Rate	0%	0%
Financial Resources Per Student	10%	10%
Average Alumni Giving Rate	5%	5%
Total	100%	100%

[*"Best Colleges Ranking Criteria and Weights"* by Robert Morse and Eric Brooks, *U.S. News & World Report*, September 9, 2018]

RED FLAG! RED FLAG!

The data that U.S. News draws upon are provided by each college.

Have you ever heard of the idiom: *'like a fox guarding the henhouse'*?

The same thing can be alluded to regarding colleges providing quantitative results – numbers – for the ratings and rankings.

There is a saying among accountants, a field assumed to be a purely numerical equation of numbers in, numbers out, that goes: *'numbers don't lie, people do.'*

There have been cases where colleges have gamed the system by providing inaccurate, even downright deceitful, numbers for the ratings game.

With higher education now being based upon a consumer model and the desire for colleges to up their rankings, there have been a number of cases where colleges provided either wrong data or gamed the system to increase their rating.

Some examples of colleges that have been caught with their proverbial hand in the cookie jar include:

- In 2012 to secure higher US News ratings of *'best'* colleges the five following colleges were caught inflating standardized test scores and class rankings for members of their incoming classes: Bucknell University, Claremont

McKenna College, Emory University, Tulane University and George Washington University.

- In the fall of 2011, Iona College admitted that its admissions staff had lied for years about test scores, freshman retention, graduation rates, student-faculty ratio, acceptance rates and alumni giving.
- In 2008, Baylor University offered financial rewards to admitted students to retake the SAT with the hope of increasing its average score.
- In 2018, Temple University admitted that its business school had submitted false data to *U.S. News & World Report* from 2015 to 2018 about its online M.B.A. program.
- In May of 2019, *U.S. News & World Report* stripped the University of Oklahoma of its ranking after the university admitted to supplying incorrect information about alumni giving since 1999.

You might think these examples, and there are more, are a handful compared to the 2000 plus colleges and universities in the U.S., but in the summer of 2012 a survey of 576 college admissions officers for Inside Higher Ed found that 91% believe other colleges had falsely reported their standardized test scores and other admissions data.

Apart from inflating scores and lying about results, there are other ways by which colleges can game the ratings / rankings system:

- Some colleges seek more applications from high school students in order to report a lower percentage of acceptance rate.

- Other colleges delay admission to low-scoring students until January thereby keeping them from being included in the averages for the class admitted in September.

In the table above, you'll note that 20% of the weighted value is given over to the school's undergraduate academic reputation. For National Universities and National Liberal Arts Colleges, three-quarters of that 20% comes from peer assessment [other colleges' views of a particular college] and one-fourth from high school counselors. For Regional Universities and Regional Colleges, the entire 20% comes from peer assessment [other colleges' view of a particular college].

This 20% of academic reputation is NOT a quantitative measure but rather a subjective assessment. AND it's assessment more on hearsay or legacy than a truly informed opinion. College administrators have enough on their plate regarding the doings of their own college and do not have the time to provide due diligence of what is going on at other colleges.

No, to some large degree these ratings and rankings are largely only ravings and rantings.

Not only is the quantitative data inaccurate due to reliance on the information submitted by the college itself. The qualitative factors are mere opinions with little basis other than general acceptance.

If you were to name *best colleges*, the ones that are likely to spring to your mind would be those considered *best* by general opinion, popular consensus.

You might come up with the typical colleges considered *'the best'*: Ivies like Yale and Harvard, or Stanford or Johns Hopkins.

Some of your *'best'* colleges might be name recognition as a result of their football program: Ohio State, Notre Dame, Alabama.

I went to the University of Pennsylvania and whenever I went back to Florida over holidays people would ask me where I was going to college. I would reply 'Penn' and they would then clarify by asking 'Penn State?' No, I didn't go to Penn State. I went to Penn, the University of Pennsylvania. At the time, Penn State's football program was coached by the legendary Joe Paterno.

Although football plays a significant, and sometimes nefarious, role in college providing strong association for alumni and consequently college donors, I'll discuss later in this book the increasingly bleak outlook for college football.

The ratings and rankings of colleges are largely subjective. The quantitative data can be fudged, as noted above, and the quantitative data can change year to year. The qualitative data are all subjective and largely based upon opinion, much of which is drawn from past experience, past accolades, the mystique heaped upon the school over the years.

One of the things that *'best colleges'* do not and cannot evaluate is the question whether that particular college or colleges is a *'good fit'*, the *'best college'* for the individual student. And that should be the key concern.

Will a specific student find themselves in the *'right'* college for them by selecting out of *Princeton Review's 'Best Colleges'* or *US News & World Report's 'Best Colleges'*?

Not too likely.

To reiterate: Rating and Rankings are only Ravings and Rantings.

CHAPTER 5   THE LIE OF THE FUTURE

One thing constantly pounded into the consciousness of the
general public is

YOU HAVE TO GO TO COLLEGE TO MAKE A
GOOD LIVING, BE SUCESSFUL AND
ENGAGE THE
AMERICAN DREAM

Authorities and commentators come up with the *'statistics'* of
the lifetime income of a college graduate versus the lifetime
income of a high school graduate. They indicate that the
lifetime earnings can be as much as 84% greater for a college
grad than a high school grad.

I often suggest to people that before they accept
pronouncements at face value they should ALWAYS

Check the Source AND Check their Agenda

As if taking whacks at a candy-filled piñata, let me forcefully
strike against some of the lies of the future income between
college grads and high school grads.

<u>A. Where is the information coming from?</u>

Often the information of the discrepancy between the lifetime earnings between high school grads and college grads comes from institutional sources and usually compiled by college grads. College departments, governmental institutions, even non-profit organizations trot out the facts and figures. Any and all of these various sources have an agenda --- an ages old belief that college is not merely important but necessary to effectively and productively work in society. Colleges want to fill their seats, non-profit organizations accept the assumption that college grads are more knowledgeable and skilled, and governmental institutions with their takeover of student loans have a vested interest in increasing the rolls of students taking out student loans. Whether intentional or not, there is an inherent bias that college makes the educated man / woman.

But is it really so?

In 2017, the 10 Richest People in the World were:

1. Jeff Bezos

2. Bill Gates

3. Amancio Ortega

4. Warren Buffet

5. Mark Zuckerberg

6. Carlos Slim Helu

7. Larry Ellison

8. Michael Bloomberg

9. Bernard Arnault

10. Charles & David Koch

Of these ten, Bill Gates, Amancio Ortega, Mark Zuckerberg and Larry Ellison never finished college

Other people who never finished college and whom you might admit were well-educated or highly successful with a happy and fulfilling life, and have made a few dollars or more include:

- Steve Jobs & Steve Wozniak of Apple

- Michael Dell of Dell Technologies

- Jan Koum of WhatsApp

- Travis Kalanick of Uber

- John Mackey of Whole Foods

- Ellen DeGeneris

- Ted Turner

- Anna Wintour

- Russell Simmons

- David Geffen

- Rachael Ray

- Paul Allen

- Sheldon Adelson

- Tom Hanks

- James Cameron

- Tiger Woods

- LeBron James

- Adele

- Lady Gaga

- Madonna

- Billy Joel

- Ralph Lauren

- Richard Branson

I could go on listing highly successful people who never finished college, but you get the point.

Despite the society emphasis upon college as the door through which one attains a happy, prosperous and successful life, that's not the only way.

In recent years, technology firms are looking beyond a college degree for their employees.

In 2017, Sam Ladah, head of IBM's talent organization, talked about *'new-collar jobs'* where applicants were now being considered not on their educational background but rather on their skills set. *["Why More Tech Companies Are Hiring People Without Degrees"*, Cale Guthrie Weissman, Fast Company, April 3, 2017].

From the same article, senior researcher at Brookings Institute, Gary Burtless stated*: "There are tons of occupations out there for which you do not need a college degree."*

As early as 2013, Google realized that college transcripts and GPAs were virtually worthless in hiring. The June 19th, 2013 issue of *The New York Times* had an interview by Adam Bryant with Laszlo Bock, then senior vice president of people operations at Google. Bock stated: *"… academic environments are artificial environments… One of my own frustrations when I was in college and grad school is that you knew the professor was looking for a specific answer. You could figure that out, but it's much more interesting to solve problems where there isn't an obvious answer. You want people who like figuring out stuff where there is no obvious answer."*

In 2011, Peter Thiel, the technology entrepreneur and investor who was involved in the start-ups for both PayPal and Facebook, founded Thiel Fellowship, which provides a $100,000 grant to accepted Fellows who are twenty-two or younger and are willing to skip or step out of college in order to build something they care about.

Although society has long held a presumed belief that a college degree is the doorway to career success, this assumption seems increasingly like the lie of the future.

In years past, apprenticeship and learning on the job were the ways of developing necessary skills. Apprenticeship is not lost and seems to be coming back in various economic sectors. Developing skills outside of college provides the necessary training through on-the-job performance or through certification programs that focus on the particular skill set.

Being saddled with thousands of dollars, tens of thousands of dollars or even hundreds of thousands of dollars in student loan debt might make sense if there were guarantees that the debt was more than worth it in future income.

Is it? Really?

Despite the college hawkers and various other institutions proclaiming that the way to a bright future is through a college education, tomorrow's economy is NOT today's economy, much less your parents' economy or your grandparents' economy.

the times they are a'changing

If you don't believe me, re-read Chapter 3.

Many of today's jobs are gone tomorrow, sourced out to robotics and artificial intelligence.

The idea of going to work for a company, being there your entire work life is relegated to your grandparents' experience. The gold watch for years of service is a relic of a distant past economic model.

Even your parents' career experience was different with people chopping and changing, often staying no longer than seven years before moving on to a different company or even a different economic sector.

But you, who are in the future economy, don't have the benefit of either.

Instead you are likely to find yourselves in the so-called

GIG ECONOMY

While you have been in high school, you may have been introduced to entrepreneurship and entrepreneur programs. Many communities have their version of *Shark Tank* where the movers and shakers in the community provide the funding, and students compete for seed money to develop their pet project.

This development [*could we call it indoctrination?*] of entrepreneurial programs in high schools seems to prepare the student for the gig economy --- an economy where either you start your own thing or you go from project to project to project rather than any stable, full time employment with an organization.

Security in a stable organization may be lacking and all bets are off regarding future employment.

Politicians often talk about jobs, creating jobs. But talk is cheap and such proclamations may truly be only spitting into the wind of the further coming changes to the economic landscape.

Even when I was in grad school, and we're talking several decades ago, company recruiters were far more interested in those students who had some experience in the workplace rather than the theoretical students with their case studies.

Hands-on!

There are various employment opportunities that do not need a college degree

In the August 22nd, 2017, program of CBS' *Moneywatch*, they listed *'The top 10 jobs for Americans without college degrees'*.

Based upon a study from Georgetown University and JP Morgan Chase, the report indicated that there were 30 million jobs for less-educated workers that paid $55,000 as a median annual wage.

The top 10 jobs for workers without a college degree with their average salary that the *Moneywatch* program listed were:

1. Broadcast Technician $42,550

2. Diagnostic Medical Sonographer $64,280

3. Electrician $52,720

4. Executive Assistant $55,860

5. Industrial Machine Repairer $49,100

6. Medical Records Technician $38,040

7. Paralegal $49,500

8. Plumber $51,540

9. Respiratory Therapist $58,670

10. Web Developer $66,130

Apart from the above listed jobs, there are many other *'middle skill'* jobs that do not require a college degree but do necessitate mastery of a trade. And in many communities throughout the country, there is a dearth of people with the skill set to fill these positions.

Some of these jobs and their top pay scale include:

Welders   [$70,000]

Mechanics [$100,000]

Machinists [$65,000]

HVAC [heating, ventilation and air conditioning] technicians

Construction workers

Some of these jobs might not appeal, and that's a primary reason for the lack of people to fill many of these positions. But the schooling in the trades and certification cost a great deal less than a college education. They also allow the individual to work sooner rather later with the opportunity cost of earning money sooner and without the debt level that many college graduates face.

As I have pointed out, the belief that some of the high-paying jobs in the *white collar* economic sector will continue in perpetuity may be one of the great lies of the future.

Robotics and AI [artificial intelligence] will replace many of the *white collar* jobs, as I indicated in Chapter 3.

College might prepare you for a certain type of employment, but does it really?

Or are those hawking a college education like the snake oil salespeople of centuries ago --- offering something that has little value but comes with an incredible cost…

If you continue to believe in the guaranteed golden value of a college education, I have a bridge to nowhere you might be interested in purchasing.

CHAPTER 6   DOWN THE RABBIT HOLE

Society has gone through dramatic changes in the last ten – twenty years. Political correctness has become the measuring factor throughout various sectors of the economy, including colleges and universities.

Part of the political correctness, accounting for past ills and seeking to make amends, has increased dramatically the administrative costs of colleges and universities.

- Compliance with regulations,

- Greater influence of the government in higher education,

- Consumer model of college education

They all bear the brunt of changing the flavor and the efficacy of a college education.

College administrators have to work with their budget and consider where to put their monies and where to cut their costs.

One of the main tenets for marketing their particular college for many schools is to focus on their athletic programs and recreational opportunities more than their academic rigor.

You might exclaim: *'say it ain't so!'*, but people's awareness of a college often revolves around a particular sport in which their college excels.

If you think of Alabama, you might immediately think of their football team.

If you think of Oklahoma or Florida, you might think of their baseball program.

If you think of UConn, you might think of their women's basketball program.

If you think of Kentucky, you might think of their men's basketball program.

And so it goes.

Sports rule

Because alumni of various colleges and universities are often more aware of their school's athletic achievements year in, year out than they are of their school's academic achievements; colleges and universities utilize the athletic program as a marketing tool to engage alumni donors.

The coaches of a college athletic team often make more, sometimes considerably more, than the professors at that particular college.

One extreme example is UCONN Women's Basketball Coach Gino Auriemma whose salary is in excess of $2 Million a year. Auriemma ranked as the highest paid state worker in Connecticut.

Auriemma is not alone and in fact doesn't even rank in the top twenty of the highest paid college coaches in 2018.

Instead, Auriemma's salary seems diminutive when compared with members of the top twenty and their annual salary, the top ten listed below:

1. Nick Saban – University of Alabama - $11,132,000

2. Dabo Sweeney – Clemson University - $8,504,600

3. John Calipari – University of Kentucky - $7,140,000

4. Jim Harbaugh – University of Michigan - $7,004,000

5. Urban Meyer – Ohio State University - $6,431,240

6. Jimbo Fisher – Florida State University - $5,700,000

7. David Shaw – Stanford University - $5,680,441

8. Rich Rodriguez – University of Arizona - $5,631,563

9. Mike Krzyzewski – Duke University - $5,550,475

10. Tom Herman – University of Texas - $5,486,316

[*Source: The QUAD, February 12, 2018*]

I mentioned that Gino Auriemma was recently considered the highest paid public employee in Connecticut. If we look at all fifty states, the highest paid public employee happens to be a coach in thirty-nine out of the fifty states.

39 out of 50

In 39 out of the 50 US states the highest paid public employee is a coach of a college or university athletic team. [*Source: "The Highest-Paid Public Employees – You Will Be Surprised, gobankingrates.com, March 13, 2018*]

You don't have to have a PhD much less a college degree or even a high school diploma to recognize the liability that where money is involved, nefarious practices can easily follow.

And so it is with college sports. With so much money invested and with the vast sums involved in potential returns through alumni donations and television rights payments, college sports practices have devolved into a shady and abusive realm.

Recruiting tactics and assistance while attending college can be heavy handed and seductive especially for those facing an otherwise uphill slog to get into college and pay for college once there.

It used to be said that for poor African-Americans there were but two ways to get out of their impoverishment: drugs and sports.

While those two avenues have broadened in recent years as society has opened more venues for minorities, sports still provides a way to *'easy street'*. That easy street may not be to the expressway of greater success, but college sports do allow athletic minority students an entry onto the ramp.

Sweet deals in college sports might seem recent, but they have gone on for a long time.

Football at colleges and universities first began with the supposition that athletic competition instills desirable traits of character in the athlete ---rigorous personal exertion and teamwork.

Unfortunately, less desirable traits became evident. Michael Mandelbaum in his book *The Meaning of Sports* [2004] alleges that the first university athletic slush fund occurred in 1879 with Columbia University paying football players.

Mandelbaum also refers to the 1932 film with the Marx Brothers called *Horse Feathers* where the plot revolves around a college president's hiring of *'students'* to play football.

While such blatant disregard of the spirit of college athletics has resulted in fines and game forfeitures, recruiting for college sports continues with various perks offered the prospective athlete student.

The NCAA [National Collegiate Athletic Association], according to their website, *"is a member-led organization dedicated to the well-being and lifelong success of college athletes."*

Fairness and integrity are key characteristics of the NCAA mission statement. To that end, the NCAA has an infractions process to resolve any case of alleged violations by a NCAA member school.

Largely because the athletic program of any college and university is a major part of that school, and a major contributory factor of donations from alumni and other school supporters to that school, violations are often rampant.

Among some of the examples of NCAA violations over the years are:

- UConn Men's Basketball Coach Kevin Ollie, who had succeeded legendary Coach Jim Calhoun, was fired in March of 2018 for *just cause*. In June of 2018, UConn and the NCAA concluded that Ollie had violated NCAA rules by having improper training sessions and by improper contact with recruits.

- In 2018 the FBI's investigation into corruption in Division 1 men's basketball programs identified more than 20 programs as possibly violating NCAA rules with cash advances and entertainment and travel expenses for college prospects and their families.

- In 2006 and 2007, an academic cheating scandal involved some 61 players in different sports at Florida State with these athletes taking an online course for which they received the test answers before taking the test and their academic work often being completed for them.

- 2005 Heisman Trophy winner, Reggie Bush, played for USC. In 2006, allegations suggested that Bush's family had received gifts in violation of NCAA rules. In 2007, a sports agent sued Bush and his family for not repaying close to $300,000 in gifts. Bush settled the case and forfeited his Heisman award.

There are other cases, many instances, of college sports programs violating NCAA rules.

But who is to blame? Is it the high school athlete being recruited that sees a way to get into a good college and get various perks for picking one school over another college? Or is it the system that values creating a dominant college sports team?

When coaches are making millions of dollars and substantially more than the college's academic personnel, we have to conclude that the college, the college administration, the college board of trustees and the college donors are all to share the blame.

Carrot & Stick

The athletes might get perks --- cash, entertainment, travel, academic assistance, etc. --- but in comparison to the coaches and the college coffers, the college athletes often come up with the short end of the stick.

College Football is a moneymaker and the compensation to college football coaches as listed above is a good indication of what a moneymaker college football is. Not only does college football entice alumni and supporters to donate to the school. In 2015-2016, the televising of college football generated $5 Billion in revenue. Add to that figure ticket sales, merchandising and donations to the schools and you have a multi-billion dollar industry.

College recruiting of high school athletes often turns out to be a carrot and stick phenomenon --- goodies to entice the high school student athlete to choose their college, followed by heavy expectations with instances of bullying and abuse once the student is in the college and on the athletic team.

When compared to the revenue to the school, the perks that college athletes receive are minimal at best and hardly compensate for the abuse and injury that college athletes often experience in their sports program.

There are various cases of abuse of college athletes:

- Pressuring the college student athlete to continue playing even after being injured, including concussions and knee injuries.

- Abusing the college student athlete verbally and physically to the point of kicking them, hurling balls at their heads, and extreme overexertion in practice.

In response to the carrot and stick phenomenon, college athletes have struck back. College athletes have tried to organize and unionize, for which they have had some success.

In 2013, Northwestern University quarterback Kain Colter began his involvement to get his fellow football players better working conditions. In 2014, Colter co-founded the College Athletes Player's Association with the intention to unionize Northwestern's team. Although a National Labor Relations Board regional director ruled in March of 2014 that the Northwestern players could unionize, that decision was unanimously overturned by the national board in 2015.

The NCAA has asserted repeatedly that it does not employ athletes since students' participation in sports is voluntary and that college athlete students attend college to get an education and not to be employed as athletes. And yet as of 2012, Northwestern scholarship football players received up to $76,000 a year to cover their tuition, college fees, books, and room and board. As of 2015, Northwestern scholarship football players received an additional amount to cover incidental costs such as child care and travel.

The issue of organized players or the unionization of college athlete students has yet to be resolved, and is an issue that may linger on and on with a chipping away of the archaic model of non-responsibility on the colleges' part and increased protection and benefits to the college athlete students.

Death By Sport

While we are hearing of fatalities of student athletes on the playing fields and while there is increasing concern for our student athletes, this is NOT a recent phenomenon.

Between 1890 and 1905, it is alleged that 330 college athletes died from injuries sustained on the football field.

A December 1905 cartoon in the *Commercial Tribune* of Cincinnati entitled *"The Grim Reaper Smiles on the Goal Posts"* highlighted deaths from injuries sustained on the gridiron.

According to *The Washington Post* [as further reported in a March 29, 2014, article by Katie Zezima *"How Teddy Roosevelt helped save football"* published in *The Washington Post*]: *"...at least 45 football players died from 1900 to October 1905, many from internal injuries, broken necks, concussions or broken backs"*.

In 1905 alone, 18 players died
playing college football

After the 1905 football season, President Theodore Roosevelt is said to have encouraged college presidents to improve the game of football and reduce the unnecessary roughness of the game. Some colleges, including Columbia, Duke and Northwestern, suspended their football program. Other colleges demanded reform of the game. Thus began steps of modification to football, how it's played and the ways that it's played.

To protect college students from dangerous and exploitive athletics practices, the Intercollegiate Athletic Association of the United States (IAAUS) was formed in 1906 with its name changed in 1910 to the National Collegiate Athletic Association (NCAA).

In 1939, the NCAA made football helmets mandatory. Subsequent improvements to football equipment included facemasks, shoulder pads, pants and shoes --- all incorporated to increase player mobility and player safety.

Despite the improvements in equipment and rules to the game of collegiate football, the game itself is injury-ridden to the athletes with liabilities of long-term effects and even death.

With football being a high impact game, a college football player can be hit in the head more than 1000 times over the course of a season. Concussions are common with repetitive hits to the head creating brain trauma and liable to CTE – Chronic Traumatic Encephalopathy, a degenerative brain disease leading to memory loss, impaired judgment, confusion and even dementia. Victims of CTE suffer depression and paranoia and may exhibit aggressive behavior even to the point of murder or suicide.

The suicides of NFL Hall of Fame linebacker Junior Seau and Pro Bowl safety Dave Duerson made national news headlines and put the issue of CTE and concussions front and center in the public's consciousness.

In the Summer of 2017 in the *Journal of American Medical Association* the director of the Boston University CTE Center, Ann McKee and her colleagues reported finding CTE in the brains of 110 of 111 former NFL players and in 48 of 53 former college players.

There are various lawsuits still pending against the NCAA by college athletes seeking damages and arguing that the NCAA knew about the liabilities of head injuries in football and did little to protect the players. The NCAA didn't even have a policy addressing concussions until 2010 and even then the policy is hardly enforced.

The NCAA did settle a class-action lawsuit in 2014 brought by former college athlete players for damages as a result of concussions received on the playing field. As opposed to compensating the individual players, the $75 million settlement is to be used for research, testing and monitoring.

College Football is a moneymaker

There are subsequent lawsuits that have been filed by individual former players for the long-term damages as a result of head injuries incurred while playing college football.

In a pamphlet put out by the National Athletic Trainers' Association published in 2018 and entitled *"At Your Own Risk: A Safer Approach to Work, Life and Sport"*, the following claims are made in regard to high school student athletes:

- *"90 PERCENT of student athletes report some sort of sports-related injury"*

- *"In 2012 alone, 163,670 MIDDLE SCHOOL OR HIGH SCHOOL ATHLETES were reported being seen in the emergency room for a concussion"*

- *"Between 2008 and 2015, more than 300 SPORTS-RELATED DEATHS of young athletes occurred in America alone"*

Not all sports-related injuries are reported and some of these injuries may have long-term effects that are not recognized at the time of the incident.

Studies of young athletes who incurred repetitive head impacts suggest a link in their adult years of developing cognitive issues such as Alzheimer's and Parkinson's.

With this information of the dangers of certain sports, and especially football, becoming public knowledge and repeated incident after incident, what has been the impact on sports in schools?

According to the National Federation of State High School Associations, participation in high school football programs peaked in 2008 at 1.11 million high school athletes. By 2017 that number had declined to 1.06 million high school athlete participants, a decline of almost 5%.

While more high schools nationwide are fielding football teams, there is a huge discrepancy geographically between increases and decreases of high school football programs. According to a *Washington Post* article by Jacob Bogage in August 2017, in the past five years states such as Oklahoma, Arkansas and Florida have added 150 football teams, while other states have seen a significant decline in high school football programs:

- Pennsylvania with a net loss of 12

- Missouri with a net loss of 24

- California with a net loss of 28

- Michigan with a net loss of 57

Add to that the pre-high school football programs with nearly a 30% drop in participation, and the future of football could be in danger --- UNLESS something is done to increase the safety of the sport and eliminate the liability of football being a crippling influence to its players to the extreme of football being a death sport.

Chapter 7:   COLLEGE LIFE

The GOOD, the BAD, and the UGLY

College is intended to educate and to mature the young adult. A college student is given greater independence than what they found in high school. They might be living away from home for the first time. Even if they are a commuter student still living in their family home, they have the chance and opportunity to greater select their course of study, especially once core requirements are met.

An incoming college student may be highly disciplined and concentrate largely on the academics of college life.

Or an incoming college student could be far more interested in the social life and freedom that college offers to the detriment of their academics in college.

Or the incoming student might find a workable balance blending both a focus on their studies and engaging the social activities of college life.

In truth, the more balanced a college student can be whereby they can balance their focus on academics with a healthy social life, the more likely they are to be successful in learning their studies and developing into a responsible and well-rounded adult.

Unfortunately, that sense of balance can be like a gymnast on a narrow balance beam --- sometimes one can make it across, other times there can be a spill off the beam.

For some college students, the stress of the academic courses becomes TOO MUCH.

The level of anxiety that a college student might feel can go extreme. Not only is the college student feeling very alone, but this sense of aloneness can quickly turn into loneliness, especially in this day and age when students from pre-k through elementary, middle and even high school have been told that they are special, have been cared for by their parents and other adults in their lives and often to a point where the child never exhibited the full emotions of life, including the sense of triumph and the agony of defeat.

Real life conditions have often been kept from children as each child was given a trophy or banner just for participating, and every child was provided a happy, safe space. Unfortunately, young children too often have been living in an illusory world that protected the child from pain or even unpleasantness.

When the young adult, although emotionally still a child, comes to college, there is the expectation of continuing to be cared for. Safe spaces, happy places are expected. Keeping the ills of humanity and the sores of the world away become paramount.

Such an unrealistic projection of life counters with the reality of college and stepping out into a larger world beyond the haven of family and local community.

Unfortunately, some children, albeit intended to be young adults, just cannot cope. The bottom falls out for them, and the liability is to escape the real world.

To maintain a connection and continue protection of their college student, some parents become what are referred to as *'velcro'* parents or *'helicopter'* parents, either stuck like glue to their child as they go through their college experience or hover around them through constant contact.

With residential real estate having become a speculative investment venture over the past few decades, some parents buy an apartment or house in the town where their child is attending college. Such a situation provides housing for their child during their college years with the additional possibility of renting out rooms to their child's college friends. After their child finishes college, the parents can continue to rent out the property to college students or can sell the property with an assumed appreciation in value of the property.

Other parents may rent housing for themselves in the town where their child is attending college to be ever present for their child, a child who chronologically is supposed to be moving into adulthood. Less attached parents may visit their college student frequently no matter how far the distance between home and the college campus.

Recent parenting has been akin to coddling [mother smothering, overprotective parenting], consequently creating a need for *'safe space'* on the college campus.

Although it was assumed that Hilary Clinton would win the US Presidency in the 2016 election, the fact that Donald Trump was elected president triggered despair and despondency among the Clinton supporting college students. To assuage their fear, colleges tried various palliatives to comfort the forlorn.

The University of Pennsylvania provided a *'breathing'* space where distraught students could go to hug a puppy, play with a cat or color on sheets of paper that had captions of positive messages. Various colleges cancelled classes and mid-term exams. Cry-ins were held at colleges, arts and crafts sessions were provided for students, and apart from coloring, some colleges offered their anxious college students Play-Doh, blowing bubbles, and other *'self-care'* modalities that would seem more attuned to young children rather than college students.

The reactions of various colleges to assuage the fear of its students to the Trump victory prompted one professor, University of Michigan-Flint business professor Mark Perry, to state:

"Institutions of higher learning have gone from being places that might best be described as 'intellectual boot-camps,' where [students] are challenged with a diversity of new ideas, to being places that might now be, more accurately, described as 'kindergartens' for adults where they are no longer challenged, but instead treated as fragile, intellectual children and coddled with a 'safe place' response to anything challenging or upsetting,"
[as quoted from *Coddling campus crybabies: Students take up toddler therapy after Trump win*, Brooke Singman, Fox News, November 17, 2016]

The sense of utter despair over the Trump election was not the first case of extreme upset by college students. A year before, a Yale University lecturer and expert in early childhood education, Erika Christakis, triggered a firestorm of outrage when she responded to a directive from the International Affairs Committee at Yale, which cautioned students against costumes of cultural appropriation or misrepresentation. In an email, Ms. Christakis questioned whether the institutional directive wasn't being too controlling and that Halloween had always been seen as a day of outlandish, outrageous, even offensive, costumes. Protesters to this email saw it as but an indication of the racial insensitivity at Yale. From the firestorm of protests Erika Christakis eventually resigned her position.

One might assume that the pampering of a college age student is right and reasonable. And certainly the coddling of children has been a large part of parenting over the past few decades. Parents have given up their responsibility in parenting and instead sought to become friends with their children. Trophies for all participants, exclaiming that each and every child is special, have contributed to the arrested development of college age students.

One result has been the increasing use of deferment in college admissions. Many colleges will accept a high school student for admission to their college or university but increasingly with the proviso of a one-year deferment, the proverbial gap year between high school and college, with the college admissions staff hope and expectation that the admitted student will more mature over the gap year.

Whether or not the college bound student has matured and grown up during that one-year deferment, statistics are troubling and may appear a condemnation of modern day parenting and the arrested emotional development of young adults.

For many college students, their course studies and the academics come with a great deal of stress, a body response that many people have difficulty managing or have not created effective ways to deal with. Part of growing up is dealing with difficulties, facing challenges and addressing stressful situations. Unfortunately, the skill set developed from successfully addressing problem areas in life has been lacking for many children as their parents have sought to protect them, enable them and keep them from the hard, cold realities of life. Although well meaning, parents have contributed to the old dictum that *the pathway to hell is paved with good intentions*.

Anxiety and depression have increased among college students. The 2015 Annual Report from the Center for Collegiate Mental Health at Penn State University studying data for the 5 years between 2010 and 2015 from an average of 100 colleges and universities and a data base of approximately 100,000 student clients found the following alarming statistics:

1. Attended counseling for mental health concerns: from 45.2% to 48.8%
2. Taken a medication for mental health concerns: from 31.0% to 33.1%
3. Been hospitalized for mental health concerns: from 7.0% to 10.2%
4. Purposely injured your self without suicidal intent: from 21.8% to 25.0%
5. Seriously considered attempting suicide: from 23.8% to 32.9%

It would be nice to say things are looking up if they weren't so down.

The suicide rate among young adults, ages 15 -24, has tripled since the 1950s, and suicide is currently the second most common cause of death among college students.

There are a multitude of causes and diverse reasons for suicide but one of the key factors is a sense of

OVERWHELM

The college student may be away from home for the first time, might have to face making decisions on their own for the first time. Their support system of parents and friends may be gone, and they might have difficulty connecting with their new community of college students. Erratic sleep patterns and disruptions to routine could prove challenging. And add to these different factors the stress of college courses.

Although some students can experience overwhelm in college, there are also great outlets for students.

Within the larger community of the college or university, there have been smaller communities such as the Greek life of fraternities and sororities.

GREEKS, NO GEEKS

Many colleges and universities have fraternities and sororities on-campus or off campus. They provide a close-knit community within the larger community of the college campus. They also provide a strong networking connection after college.

It is estimated that some 750,000 college students belong to a fraternity or sorority with a total of 9 million student and alumni members.

Advocates of Greek life draw upon the studies showing that fraternity and sorority members compared to non-Greek life college students are more likely to graduate on time and are likely to earn higher salaries in their career. Greek organizations often do volunteer work in the local community and raise monies for charities.

While advocates of Greek life have solid points to make their case, Greek organizations in recent years have come under increased criticism with charges of elitism and nepotism, excessive alcoholism and partying, sexism and sexual assault, racism and discriminatory.

For those first year college students looking to join a fraternity or sorority there is a rushing and pledging process where students visit the different fraternities for men, sororities for women, to see whether they feel a match to that particular Greek organization. After the initial recruitment phase, the fraternity / sorority members determine whom they will invite to become a member. If the chosen applicant accepts the invitation, the first year student has pledged to that particular fraternity or sorority and enters a pledge period that may culminate in some form of hazing, which runs from mild humiliation to downright abuse with some extremes having resulted in the pledge's death during hazing.

The classic movie *Animal House* provided a madcap romp of the extreme antics of one particular fictional college fraternity.

In an article in the October 13th, 2017, issue of *The Economist* entitled *"Hazing deaths on American college campuses remain far too common"*, it is reported from data compiled by Professor Hank Nuwer of Franklin College that since 1838 more than 200 university students had died from hazing-related accidents in the United States and 40 such deaths between 2007 and 2017. The main cause of these deaths has been related to alcohol poisoning.

The use and abuse of alcohol and drugs are not limited to the Greek life on college campuses. Apart from academics, college life celebrates good times through partying, which invariably includes alcohol, drugs, sex and… *whatever gets you through the night s'alright, s'alright…"* [to borrow from John Lennon].

According to a report on college drinking by the National Institute on Alcohol Abuse and Alcoholism:

> *"Factors related to specific college environments also   are significant. Students attending schools with strong Greek systems and with prominent athletic programs tend to drink more than students at other types of schools. In terms of living arrangements, alcohol consumption is highest among students living in fraternities and sororities and lowest among commuting students who live with their families."*

This same report drew upon a 2014 National Survey on Drug Use and Health to provide the following statistic: Approximately 60% of college students between the ages of 18 and 22 drank alcohol in the prior month with almost 2 out of 3 of them binge drinking.

The National Institute on Alcohol Abuse and Alcoholism also reported that:

1. about 696,000 students between the ages of 18 and 24 are assaulted by another student who has been drinking

2. about 97,000 students between the ages of 18 and 24 report experiencing alcohol-related sexual assault or date rape.

Sex, drugs, and rock 'n' roll

may have been the rallying cry of the counterculture in the 1960s, but today is not much different. Where a difference lies is that the 1960s were more about peace, love and groovy feelings. The 2010s seem a great deal more harsh and edgier, but edgier in a mean-spirited way.

Sexual intimacy is often a large part of the college experience. Although students are likely to have had sexual encounters prior to college, college life promotes greater ease and opportunity for sexual involvements. Hormones are raging and can be fuelled by the desire for greater intimacy and loosened by the ingestion of drink or drugs.

Consensual sex is one thing and fully understandable among young adults, but sexual assault and rape are a totally different matter. Unfortunately, as reported by the organization RAINN [Rape, Abuse & Incest National Network] sexual violence on college campuses is widespread:

23% of female college undergraduate students experienced sexual assault or rape

And these are reported incidents. It is estimated that only one-fifth of sexual assaults are reported to enforcement authorities and is the LEAST often reported violent crime.

Why would such assaults go unreported?

There can be various reasons that sexual assaults go unreported, including:

- fear of embarrassment

- fear of not being believed

- fear of efficacy in the campus justice system

- fear of efficacy in the criminal justice system

- fear of the alleged assailant

- fear of having provoked or somehow invited the assault

Most sex crimes are NEVER reported

At one time, drugs were embraced for consciousness-expanding. The 1960s were a time of peace, love, brotherhood, idealism, free sex, and lots of mind-altering drugs.

Today, drugs seem a panacea to the ills of the world and all the discomforts that people personally feel. Whether recreational drugs or prescription drugs, the use and abuse of drugs in the United States have reached epidemic proportions.

We virtually raise our children on drugs. According to the US Centers for Disease Control and Prevention, close to 24%, not quite one-fourth, of all children under the age of 18 in the US take at least one prescription medication each month. These prescribed medicines include antidepressants, anti-anxiety, ADD or ADHD, opioids and other psychotropic medications.

We are one highly medicated population, and we have introduced our children to this way of life.

It's always amazing to watch on television the pharmaceutical ads with their inspiring message of help and hope, their soothing music and joyous sense, and buried at the end in a fast, hardly discernible, patter the list of liable negative, even life-threatening, side-effects of taking the particular drug.

Should we be surprised by the negative impacts our drugged-out society incurred after feeding our children, ourselves, pill after pill after pill?

In the musical group Jefferson Airplane's song *White Rabbit* written by lead singer Grace Slick, the lyrics go:

"One pill makes you larger, and one pill makes you small
And the ones that mother gives you, don't do anything at all
Go ask Alice, when she's ten feet tall"

In discussing the song that was released in 1967 and picked by *Rolling Stone* magazine in 2011 as one of the *500 Greatest Songs of All Time*, Grace Slick said:

"Our parents read us stories like Peter Pan, Alice in Wonderland and The Wizard of Oz. They all have a place where children get drugs, and are able to fly or see an Emerald City or experience extraordinary animals and people... And our parents are suddenly saying, 'Why are you taking drugs?' Well, hello!"

According to the US government's Health and Human Services department in 2016:

* 11.5 million people misused prescription opioids
* 2.1 million people had an opioid use disorder
* 42,249 people died from overdosing on opioids
* 948,000 people used heroin

Whether already addicted prior to entering college or not, the college experience with its freedom of individual choice, peer pressure and a desire for *'good times'* provides fertile ground for drug use and alcohol abuse. The consequences can be varied and extreme, pushing the envelope to the point of being on the edge. But who will step in to curb the potentially lethal effects of alcohol and / or drug use? The answer frankly is

NO ONE

A DREAM... NO MORE...

One of the most inspiring historic speeches was given by Dr. Martin Luther King, Jr. on August 28th, 1963, and entitled *'I Have a Dream'*, in which Dr. King called out:

"I have a dream that one day… little black boys and black girls will be able to join hands with little white boys and white girls as sisters and brothers."

SEGREGATION
         INTEGRATION
                  VOLUNTARY
SEGREGATION

Part of the college experience, and a rallying cry for those in the education field, is and has been emphasis on diversity.

Diversity has been extolled as a major influence in college… diversity of opinion… diversity of backgrounds of the college community incorporating students diverse in cultural background, ethnicity and economic strata.

Although colleges may have been started to train ministers and later the elites before becoming democratized with the idea of *'college for all'*, recent trends have accelerated the diversity in the college community BUT without the assimilation of the diverse groups within the college community.

On the contrary, like minds, similar characteristics have created an almost like *'circling the wagons'* mentality whereby people seek out people similar to themselves. Foreign students may congregate with other students from their same national identity. Frat and sorority students may stay within their organization community. African-American, black, students may socialize with each other. Similar to the larger community in our towns and our cities whereby *'same'* populations --- whether cultural, ethnic or racial --- stay together, the college experience which was to open the individual students to a larger, more diverse world within their college community has denigrated into students of one particular demographic group hanging with other students of the same demographic group.

This tendency has morphed on some college campuses into demands and accommodations for group housing of like students.

Honor houses where honors college scholars live provide fertile ground for highly motivated students to share in discussions, study groups and recreation. These are living learning communities.

Over the past few years, black student groups have called for separate college dorm housing for black students. Some colleges have acceded to students' demands and created separate dorm housing for blacks. Critics condemn the move saying that such colleges are sending the wrong message that segregation is okay. Supporters of the move suggest that it's no big deal since colleges often have *'themed'* housing of like-minded students. At some colleges and universities, the separate but equal themed-housing has included organizing dormitory housing by race, ethnicity, sexual orientation, and other specified identity housing.

Despite society's attempts at social engineering towards inclusion, reality suggests a tendency towards self-segregation both in the larger community and on college campuses. People tend to prefer being with people that are the same or at least similar to them, whether that sameness is translated into cultural, ethnic, intellectual, political or sexual sameness.

One thing that seems to be the same with colleges recently is the rush towards improving the amenities on the college campus.

EDUCATION OR COUNTRY CLUB

In times past, college was seen as a forum for education with the emphasis placed upon the academics. That period of time was when a college education was less expensive and when the college administration dictated the ways and wherefores of the college experience.

Those times are past with a shift in the college education moving from an education model to a consumer model.

With the cost of a college education running into the equivalent of buying a house and a college education no longer being on average a four-year experience but being dragged out to as many as six years, colleges have increasingly sought to entice the prospective student to their campus by means of amenities, the fun stuff that students have become accustomed to.

While parents used to parent their children and adhered to strict *'do's and don'ts'* of what children could do and could not do, recent parenting has had parents abdicate their role and allowed the child, not the parent, to dictate the rules.

Instead of the more authoritarian role of parenting in times past, parents have become *'friends'* to their children and have sought to protect their child[ren] from harsh realities of living. Competition has given way to participation where the emphasis is no longer on a win-lose proposition but rather a celebration of engagement. Working towards accomplishment and achievement has been usurped by entitlement and a sense of deserving without exertion.

In keeping with this transition in lifestyle especially acute in the US, colleges and universities in the US have marketed their schools by emphasizing the lifestyle amenities more than the academic rigor.

 In what Forbes magazine in its July 31, 2014 issue, referred to as the *"College Amenities Arms Race"*, colleges have dramatically increased their expenditures and their investment in offering pleasing, even luxuriant, recreational activities, some of which include:

- a *"Leisure Pool"* in the university's aquatic center with a water park of a 64-foot long lazy river, a diving well and water slide, a wet deck for tanning, a 25-person hot tub, and a poolside cafe [Texas Tech]
- a first-class restaurant, the 1924 Prime Steakhouse, a movie theater with complimentary popcorn, a free arcade, a free ice cream truck, and puppy study breaks [High Point University]
- a 240,000 square-foot rec center with the nation's longest indoor running track, a 45-person hot tub and a five-story rock climbing wall [Auburn University]
- a *'relaxation room'* with high-tech napping pods [Saint Leo University]
- a fitness center with a golf simulator, a climbing wall, high-end juice bars, a co-ed sauna and an Olympic sized swimming pool [University of Pennsylvania]

These colleges are not alone in their offerings to students, only an example of the amenities colleges are offering their students in the *'consumer as king'* model that higher education has become.

College life has become a myriad of experiences and like life itself entails the good, the bad, and the ugly.

Chapter 8:   SNOWFLAKES TO SLUSH

Like a snowflake, each one of us is unique. Unfortunately, the term *'snowflake'* has taken on a pejorative term, referring to someone who thinks they are special, unique and wanting to hear only what agrees with them. Today's snowflake seems easily offended, hurt, fearful of the harsh realities of the world and in pursuit only of happy, safe spaces.

With colleges focused on the consumer model of education, colleges have bent over backwards to accommodate not only the needs but also the desires of the consumer --- the college student.

Only recently have terms such as *'micro-aggressions'* and *'trigger warnings'* become part of the lexicon of education --- in elementary school, secondary school, and college.

Nothing to offend

College used to be an arena in which to explore ideas, discuss topics and confront thoughts opposite to one's own beliefs.

By considering both the thesis and the antithesis of a topic, one could arrive at a synthesis and in the process develop critical thinking.

At one time, this was the model of education. Students would be asked to present their argument, face the criticism of those who disagreed with their viewpoint, and then rebut the criticism. This process was once the foundation stone of education, deepened the student's understanding of the issue and sharpened their thought processes. That was education in an earlier time before society decided not to present anything that would hurt or offend anyone.

This trend towards avoiding antagonistic remarks is a form of political correctness. Political correctness is more accurately perceived as censorship, closing down opposing viewpoints and creating a very narrow perspective from which to view what is considered by the consensus as *'right'* and *'true'*… although *'right'* is not the right word for the college experience, but we'll get to that shortly.

In this effort to avoid hurting or offending any one of their students, educators have incorporated what are referred to as *'trigger warnings'*. A trigger warning is an alert to the student that the content might prove distressing and emotionally upsetting. Huh? What hath parents and our society wrought?

Avoiding upset, avoiding distress?

To assume that life is just a walk in the park without challenges, brambles or upsets is totally unrealistic and **NOT** what life, living, education, growth and development are all about. Only in a heavily medicated and sedated society can we hope to avoid upset and distress, and even then the dosage or medication may have to be adjusted to numb the liable pain of doing life.

Included in his welcoming letter to the incoming freshmen
to the University of Chicago in 2016, the Dean of Students
wrote:

> *"Our commitment to academic freedom means*
> *that we do not support so-called "trigger warnings",*
> *we do not cancel invited speakers because their*
> *topics might prove controversial, and we do not*
> *condone the creation of intellectual "safe spaces"*
> *where individuals can retreat from ideas and*
> *perspectives at odds with their own."*

In response, more than 150 faculty members at the
University of Chicago published a letter criticizing efforts to
prohibit *"trigger warnings"*.

Perhaps one can make the case of warnings such as *'watch
out', 'be careful', 'dangerous curve ahead'* for driving, hiking,
biking and other forms of physical movement. BUT for
readings and studies?

Trigger warnings just do not make sense and instead create a
climate whereby expressions need to be incredibly vanilla not
to upset anyone or create any level of distress.

Can we call it the numbing and dumbing down?

If we accept only those things that are palatable to us, then
we are putting on blinders and seeing only what we want to
see, read only what we want to read, hear only what we want
to hear. In the process, we close ourselves off to a wide
palette of knowledge, information, discourse and discussion.

Tied in with this recent employment of trigger warnings, concern has been raised about micro aggressions. Not aggressions or violent expressions but microaggressions. We all understand what aggressive behavior is like, but what the hell are microaggressions?

According to the *Merriam-Webster Dictionary*, microagression is defined as:

"a comment or action that subtly and often unconsciously or unintentionally expresses a prejudiced attitude toward a member of a marginalized group (such as a racial minority)"

You have to love the concept that a microaggression is *'subtle'* and that it might be something expressed that is either unconscious or unintentional.

With *'trigger warnings'* and microaggressions it would seem necessary to bring in the **THOUGHT POLICE**, the arbiter of what is truly some form of aggression, no matter how micro or minimal it might seem. And, of course, we need to discern what warrants *'trigger warnings'* and what doesn't.

Unfortunately, people may be so thin-skinned that they can easily take offense to anything and virtually everything, thereby closing themselves off to the unpleasantness of discord and even disagreement.

And that's where we have come --- to a homogenized world dictated by...... ????

Political Correctness

The question of balance is also tied into the concept of gaining greater understanding of an issue or a problem. As mentioned previously, true education comes about from considering the thesis and the antithesis to arrive at a synthesis that may make up elements of both thesis and antithesis but might be more comprehensive than either the thesis or the antithesis. Knowledge comes about from delving into a subject and looking at different facets to discern the essence and true substance of the matter.

Otherwise, and is often the case in college education today, we are being served pablum.

With the strength of the p.c. [political correctness] culture imposing its opinions and views as being the true reality, it might be wise to consider what that reality is and from where it derives.

First, let's recognize that most college educators have lived their lives in one arena --- the pastoral fields of education. From their cloistered ivory towers, they have opined on reality and a reality as they see it while safely protected by a moat surrounding their college walls.

In such hallowed halls, theory trumps experience, the idling of the mind considered more worthy than the sweat of the hands-on.

Should it surprise anyone that the overwhelming political conviction of college educators tends towards the Liberal as opposed to the conservative? I capitalized Liberal for in truth such Liberals are not really liberal and are far from being tolerant, which the term liberal often refers.

While politics has little influence in the sciences, political affiliation may have a far greater influence in the liberal arts colleges [again liberal not Liberal, although a recent study might utilize either the lower case or upper case in the word liberal to refer to the colleges of the humanities].

Published on April 24th, 2018, in the National Association of Scholars, Mitchell Langbert, associate professor of business management at Brooklyn College, explained large discrepancy in political affiliation of college educators in his article *"Homogeneous: The Political Affiliations of Elite Liberal Arts College Faculty"*.

Drawing upon a study of 8,688 tenure track, PhD professors from 51 of the top 66 liberal arts colleges as ranked by the *US News* in 2017, Langbert found that the ratio of Democrats to Republicans among faculty members was over 10 to 1, 10 Democrats to 1 Republican.

Should this discrepancy be concerning?

Langbert writes: *"Political homogeneity is problematic because it biases research and teaching and reduces academic credibility."*

Although there are some liberal arts colleges that have adopted a viewpoint diversity strategy as did Claremont McKenna early on, the lack of diversity in liberal arts colleges is appalling, especially since it is the capital L Liberals who call for diversity. Of course, their desire for diversity is of a different kind and rarely extends to diversity in political thought.

Langbert's study of political homogeneity in liberal arts colleges are brought out by the figure and table he includes in his article:

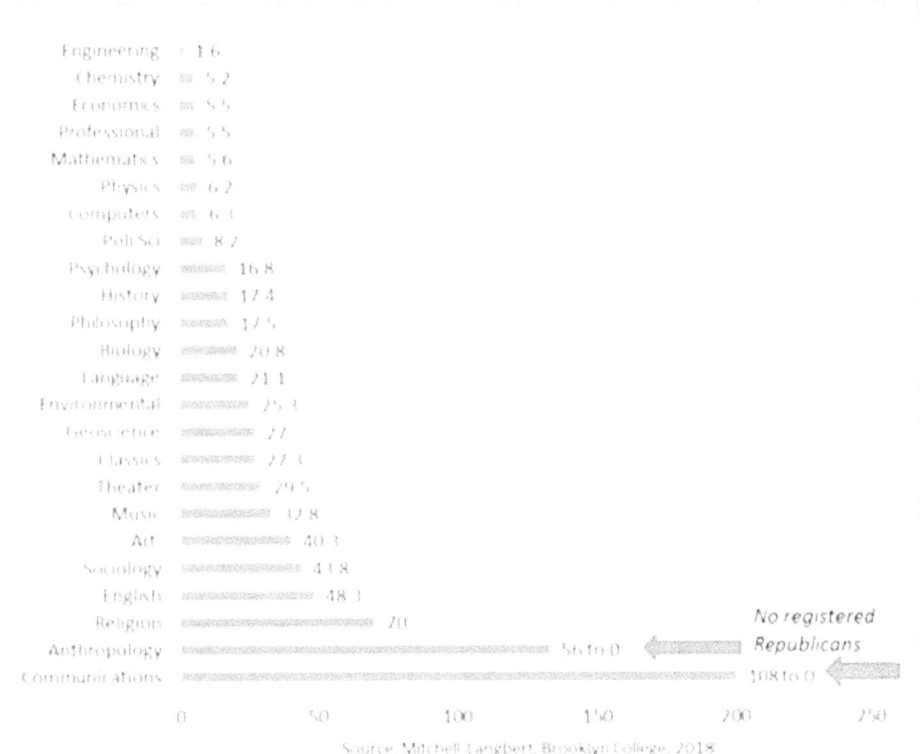

Figure 1

Number of Democratic Faculty Members for Every Republican in 25 Academic Fields

Table 1   D:R Ratios by College

Bryn Mawr	Bates	Colgate	St. Lawrence	Denison
72:0	37.5:1	19.1:1	11.8:1	4.4:1
Soka	Vassar	Colorado	Gettysburg	Claremont McK.
20:0	35:1	18.7:1	11.6:1	3.7:1
Wellesley	Amherst	Grinnell	Scripps	St. John's (MD)
136:1	34:1	18.4:1	10:1	2.9:1
Williams	Smith	Oberlin	Davidson	Kenyon
132:1	32.8:1	15.6:1	9.7:1	2.7:1
Swarthmore	Wesleyan	Haverford	Dickinson	Annapolis
120:1	31:1	15.5:1	8.7:1	2.3:1
Barnard	Connecticut	Skidmore	Bucknell	West Point
98:1	26.3:1	15.5:1	7.9:1	1.3:1
Sarah Lawrence	Hamilton	Franklin Marshall	Centre	Thomas Aquinas
54:1	24.8:1	15.4:1	6.7:1	0:26
Bowdoin	Pitzer	Occidental	Berea	
53.5:1	21.3:1	13.3:1	6.4:1	
Mount Holyoke	Union	Holy Cross	Harvey Mudd	
44.5:1	19.6:1	13:1	6.1:1	
Pomona	Trinity	Muhlenberg	Lafayette	
39.7:1	19.4:1	13:1	6.1:1	
Hobart & W.S.	Bard	Colby	Wooster	
38.3:1	19.3:1	12.1:1	5.8:1	

Sample size = 5,197. Significance level <.0001 for the chi-square test of association.

Hardly necessary to explain, the largest discrepancy Langbert found between Democrat and Republican faculty members were in interdisciplinary studies. In gender studies, peace studies and Africana studies, Republicans were an extinct breed, there wasn't one.

And what does a student get from his courses in the humanities? Perhaps, nothing more than a slanted perspective on humanity.

REEDUCATION U.

News reports and articles have often lambasted communist countries and dictatorial societies for their reeducation camps, often forced labor camps where the intransigent citizens to the accepted doctrine of that particular society are *'taught'* the evil of their ways and are re-educated to comply with the political correctness of their leaders.

The bizarro world of twenty-first century college education is that the most Liberal college professors are often the most intolerant of any view other than their own.

If a high school student has developed a healthy skepticism, questioning everything and putting various ideas under the microscope of their critical thinking; this same form of thinking might be to their detriment in college with the liability of their acquiescing to the professor's stature and getting in line with the *'correct'* opinion being espoused in class.

Needless to say, in order to do well in a class, especially in today's higher education arena, the key strategy is the proverbial *'preach to the choir'*.

Massaging the professor's ego by affirming his / her / trans stance tends to benefit the student more than confronting the professor's position with a well considered argument and well developed case opposed to the preferred opinion.

With young adults developing through their college experience, physically, emotionally and intellectually, they have a tendency to be open, even impressionable and vulnerable, to information that might be new to them or unfamiliar.

Recognizing the importance to impress the professor and seeking validation for their stance so as not to question their own integrity, college students can hew the line presented. While we could say this is education, perhaps in truth it is a form of re-education, even brainwashing, whereby a particular flavor to a topic or a specific spin on a subject is repeated often enough that the student assumes it to be the gospel truth.

DIVERSITY, TO A POINT

There are signs, bumper stickers and clarion calls to

CELEBRATE DIVERSITY

Unfortunately,

We don't see a great deal of diversity in the humanities courses of liberal arts colleges taught by strongly Liberal professors.

We don't see a great deal of diversity in the true interaction on college campuses as *'like'* students stay with *'like'* students to the point of voluntary segregation.

We don't see a great deal of diversity in the acceptance of people stepping out of their own defined characteristics and trying on a different cultural, ethnic, or religious experience… for if you do, you are likely to be accused of

CULTURAL APPROPRIATION

Instead of spreading our wings, broadening our expanse and exploring elements of life beyond our own familiar characteristics, today's society and today's higher education are narrowing the parameters and enforcing a strait jacket in our speech, in our actions, in our investigations and consequently in our very **BEING**.

In times past, higher education helped the student to take off the blinders of their narrow, parochial experiences. For many students, college was the first time they ventured beyond the confines of their familiar environment --- leaving their local community, stepping away from their friends who had been part of their *'like'* experience and moving out from the womb-like space of their family home.

Like a horse with blinders when the blinders are removed and the horse can look not merely at what is strictly ahead of them but rather can look round, look all around; students going off to college had the opportunity of being exposed to a much larger world than that with which they were familiar. Their college studies were far less regimented than their high school studies and provided them with the possibility of exploring a wide topic of subject matters. Their college classmates incorporated other students from different backgrounds, different cultures, different experiences.

College broadened the perspective and the experience of the college student… until

Political correctness got in the way

Although studies abroad and interactions with other students of a different background provided a greater understanding of differences between individuals, unique characteristics of life from a different experience and viewpoint; in recent days such exploration by a student has been castigated as *'cultural appropriation'*.

While the horse with blinders removed could look all around and see life from even a peripheral viewpoint, putting the blinders back on the horse narrows its vision and limits its perspective to only that which is straight ahead of it.

So too has the cries of cultural appropriation put blinders on the college student. No longer can a college student explore and investigate the qualities of *'difference'* by taking on the characteristics of a different culture. In today's political correctness culture, such a student is accused of cultural appropriation and framed more in the age old condemnation of the *'white man's burden'*, a phrase from a poem by Rudyard Kipling that indicated the supposed duty of the western nations' white colonizers to educate and acculturate the indigenous peoples of their colonized lands.

On the one hand, higher education is supposed to broaden a student's perspective. On the other hand, politically correct society and its offspring of higher education today limit the parameters that a student or any person can explore.

Some examples of the ridiculousness of cultural appropriation include:

1. the University of Ottawa in Canada cancelled a university yoga class over oppression concerns under the guise of cultural appropriation.
2. A caucasian High School student in Utah was chastised for wearing a Chinese dress to her 2018 prom.
3. In 2017 Kooks Burritos, a Mexican food cart in Portland, Oregon, run by two white women closed down after it was *'outed'* for culturally appropriating their recipes from Mexican women.

There are countless examples of what some people would term *'cultural appropriation'*. To some degree, cultural appropriation is a form of assimilation, an appreciation of another culture other than one's own and the proverbial *'melting pot'* of different cultures, different backgrounds coming together under one big tent.

This recent focus on cultural appropriation is but another form of segregation, self-imposed segregation whereby we stick with mine, an exclusive format that blocks out others who are different or who threaten the exploitation of *'mine'*.

During these times when we *'celebrate diversity'* too many people accept diversity as long as it stays beyond our parameters and out of our exclusive domain of *'likeness'* and *'sameness'*.

Where have we gotten?

College no longer offers the basic training in preparation of stepping out into the world and being an adult with all of its challenges and opportunities that truly living adult life encounter.

Unfortunately, the personal beauty and the true potential of an individual like the uniqueness of a snowflake under the present environment of college

turns the snowflake into slush

Chapter 9: TASTE OF ASHES

Conditioned into getting trophies, plaques, banners, gold stars, stickers, and the like for just participating, students graduating from college get the college degree paper for participating and little else.

After four to six years spent getting their college degree and liable to racking up huge student loan debt, the college graduate has largely been warehoused for those four to six years with little to show for it except possibly

political correctness conditioning

and a

scrap of paper

While in times past a college education developed critical thinking skills and the ability to coherently express personal thoughts all the while taking into consideration the pros and cons [the thesis and antithesis] of an idea or argument in order to arrive at the synthesis of a greater truth; today's college education graduate is liable to be severely lacking in some of the rudimentary skills of thought, analysis and expression.

Increasingly, earlier education is doing away with teaching students cursive writing, preferring instead print or the word processing of a computer language. Perhaps we'll get back to people making the mark of X used years ago by the illiterate as a legal signature.

Education today has become a failed model. And college education is reflective of education's failure.

There has been an assumption, and one based in fact in the past, that a college education is the highway to success --- a good job, financial prosperity, and a happy life. This belief continues to be promoted not as mere belief but as the gospel truth by the college marketers, by government, by economic sectors and as requisites for certain professions.

As I have pointed out in earlier pages, college students and students intending to go the college route have been sold a

LIE

Not only is the economy of the future less labor intensive, meaning fewer jobs for more people. And that's not only the manufacturing sector of the economy. I pointed out how the advance of Artificial Intelligence and Robotics is changing the wide palette of the economy --- from manufacturing, to the service economy, to the white collar management workers and to all the professions. The entire gamut of the economy is transforming and leaving behind much of the potential work force.

Have colleges and universities been adept at adapting their curriculum to these changing times? The answer largely is a resounding

NO

Instead of preparing the college graduate for the real world, college education has maintained a safe space for the college student and offered little to the student's skill set in preparation to work in the real world. College education has morphed from true education into political correctness conditioning. College has become an insidious engagement, saddling many students with onerous student loan debt, an albatross that lasts for years, even decades, after college graduation and an impediment to wider choice of future options. And the skills that were expected to be taught and to be developed during a college education are sorely lacking.

Reading, writing and arithmetic

These three subjects were the basics of elementary school education, the basics of education. While one would assume that students entering college and graduating college would have perfected, or at least met, a competency level in these subjects, the truth is that

It just ain't so

In a January 1ˢᵗ, 2018, article on mba.com entitled *'Employers Seek Communication Skills in New Hires'* by the GMAC Research Team, the 2017 survey by GMAC [Graduate Management Admission Council] of nearly 1000 employers who recruit on business school campuses found that communication skills top the list of the attributes employers are looking for in their prospective employees.

The results of the survey are given in the graph following

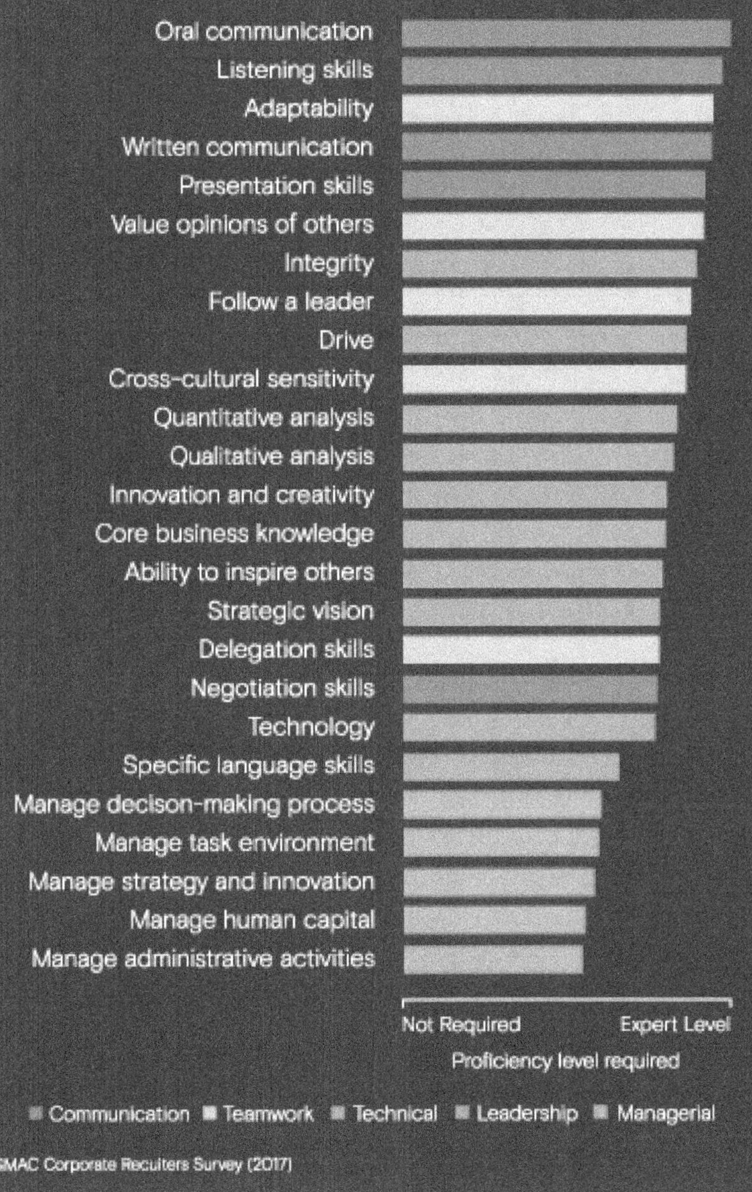

What Employers Want from New Hires
Employer rating of skill proficiency required to be placed in a mid-level position
Oral communication
Listening skills
Adaptability
Written communication
Presentation skills
Value opinions of others
Integrity
Follow a leader
Drive
Cross-cultural sensitivity
Quantitative analysis
Qualitative analysis
Innovation and creativity
Core business knowledge
Ability to inspire others
Strategic vision
Delegation skills
Negotiation skills
Technology
Specific language skills
Manage decison-making process
Manage task environment
Manage strategy and innovation
Manage human capital
Manage administrative activities
Not Required
Expert Level
Proficiency level required
Communication
Teamwork
Technical
Leadership
Managerial
GMAC Corporate Recuiters Survey (2017)

And how well do college graduates measure up in matching the expectations of prospective employers?

Not well at all.

"Surveys of employers paint a picture of discontent. Executives and hiring managers report that they have trouble finding candidates who communicate well." Education Week, October 4, 2018, *"What Literacy Skills Do Students Really Need for Work?"* by Catherine Gewertz.

One college professor, Dr. Oliver Dreon, reported in his article *"Literacy Levels Among College Students"* [*Faculty Focus*, April 17th, 2017]:
"…I was really confounded by my students' trouble with reading for deep understanding. While I could see that the students were completing assigned readings, they weren't always able to process the information deeply to analyze the concepts or apply the content to new situations."

The ability to not only read the words written but to comprehend and understand what is being conveyed is lacking in many college students and even college graduates.

In touring college campuses, I am often amazed as to how few students actually use the college library, much less, having actually walked into the library. I understand that we live in a new age, an information age, where information is available and current on the Internet. Despite the information overload on the Internet, reading something and understanding what the information means can be totally disparate.

If we have not developed critical analysis, the skill of reading something with the ability of considering the pros and cons of the case presented in the information, then we are likely to accept what we are reading, what is being told to us, at face value without questioning whether we are truly reading fact or fiction. Such a situation borders on the moronic and is a mere step away from being mental automatons --- mimicking thoughts with buzzwords or buzz phrases and no intelligent consideration of what we are saying.

We assume and are led to believe that evolution is a straight-line progression with things getting better all the time.

Sorry! Ain't necessarily so!

When people are reduced to gutteral sounds or hackneyed phrases, they may be communicating on a very base level but certainly not on a very intelligent level. Perhaps instead of evolving, our society is devolving and we are becoming stupider and stupider as time goes on. If that is the case, we can thank the models of parenting and education that have come into practice over the recent times.

In their book *Academically Adrift: Limited Learning on College Campuses,* authors Richard Arum and Josipa Roksa found that *"45 percent of 2,300 students at 24 colleges showed no significant improvement in critical thinking, complex reasoning and writing by the end of their sophomore years."* [As reported by John G. Maguire in *The Washington Post* issue of April 27, 2017, in the article *"Why so many college students are lousy at writing – and how Mr. Miyagi can help"* by Valerie Strauss]

Meeting with college students in many different colleges around the country, I have found it extraordinary how few students have had to write papers for their classes. And if they did have to write a paper, the paper may have been only five or ten pages in length. No in-depth papers, no thesis, no capstone written project --- such *scholarly* assignments are of a bygone college era.

Even Ph.D. dissertations may be brief commentaries without in-depth research done.

Where have we gotten?

We have arrived at the consumer model of education with the consumer as king and the educator as mere facilitator. We have devolved into a business model of higher education:

you pay your money,
you get your degree

And who suffers from this cavalier attitude of higher education?

[1] The individual who has spent considerable money, taken on considerable debt, has the piece of paper indicating a college degree but without the skill set to be functional and effective in the real world.

[2] Society, which is dependent upon young people taking the place of older people in maintaining the productive nature of the economy, the community, the society and the nation.

[3] Culture with enlightenment and inspiration and sophistication usurped by the crass, brash rudeness of base instincts and slightly intelligible thought processes.

Although society has placed greater emphasis on a college education, education in the US has increasingly underperformed in so many different ways.

Because of the focus on the consumer model in education, we are raising generations of illiterates with the result of college graduates who are multi-illiterate.

Not only have critical thinking, sharp analysis and clear communication in college graduates declined significantly. We also have generations of college graduates who have little knowledge of civics and the state of their nation, much less their environment. The lack of literacy in history and historical patterns begs the concern of what many commentators have cautioned:

*those who don't know history
are doomed to repeat it*

Even in our own lives, we too often don't learn our lessons. We go through life oblivious, caroming from one experience to another to yet another, without giving thought, much less scrutiny, in how our life is going, what we are doing with our living, and whether we have grown, developed and matured through life's various incidents, opportunities and challenges.

We are being numbed and dumbed down with many of us becoming little other than passive observers to the march of time, the parade of history, the active participation in our governmental structures.

Lacking understanding of civics, people tend to accept the marketing phrases, the hype of whatever appeals to them. Without clear thinking, or critical analysis or understanding of the many factors involved in a particular matter, people can be led by slogans and *'feel good'* rhetoric.

It boggles the mind as to how ill-informed people are regarding their government, the branches of government and the systems involved in the mechanics of various government institutions.

Instead, people are led by slogans and catch phrases that have little more than a means to capture the support of the ill-informed populace. Once these slogans and catch phrases have gained their advocacy, the sloganeers feel no real compulsion to act in accord with the sentiment of their slogans.

Increasingly, people feel that they no longer have control, much less impact, upon their personal lives. Things are decided for them. The powers-that-be pull the strings in accord with their own whims and wishes. There is little thought as to how choices and decisions made are likely to impact the general populace or contribute to the greater good. On the contrary, the powers-that-be are largely interested in how directions benefit their own personal good, their own personal fortune[s].

Literacy takes all forms and impacts all significant aspects of our lives.

While one would assume that education is designed and founded upon the principles of turning the illiterate into the literate, in today's reality nothing could be further from the truth.

Despite secondary school education and a higher education that culminates in a college degree, the *'learned'* individual has been passed through the different grades, the various classes and the education curriculum without gaining literacy --- literacy in critical thinking, literacy in clear and studied communication, literacy in how their government works, even literacy in finances and how the individual can deal with the economics of daily functioning.

It is staggering that many *'well educated'* individuals have such little knowledge about economics and finances.

The concepts of supply and demand, the effects of fiscal and monetary policy, the costs of credit and loans; all of these areas of finance and economics, and so many more, are largely lost on the *'educated'* individual.

On the contrary, education has dwelt more upon the *'trendy'* courses and curriculum of gender studies, ethnic studies, marketing trysts and the like --- a lot of pablum that offers little more than comic book diversions from truly life-affirming tools and a productive skill set.

It is staggering that in the US, a country of incredible bounty and opportunity, so few people know how to effectively handle money.

The belief and acceptance and the marketing ploys all perpetuate the sentiment of

IMMEDIATE GRATIFICATION

While generations before us believed in *'saving for a rainy day'*, that attitude has been lost to *'I want it now. I want it right now'*.

The snake oil salespeople of today promise easy credit, ways by which the consumer can get today what he wants without having to pay until tomorrow, or the day after. Offers of easy credit have resulted in people no longer emphasizing the importance of *'saving for a rainy day'*.

According to the St. Louis Federal Reserve, the personal savings rate in 2018 was 7.6% compared to 11.2% in 1982 and forecast to be 5.37% in 2019.

Instead of teaching people the necessity of having money put aside for emergencies or for future purchases, the hucksters have been out pushing easy credit with various *'buy it now'* schemes. And who are these hucksters? The hucksters in our society are virtually anyone and everyone who has something to sell --- from the government, to the mega corporations, to the small businesses, to colleges and universities, and to the itinerant grifters selling something, anything.

As the government's tentacles capture more and more influence over our nation's economic sectors, government agencies often become like the *Wizard of* Oz screen presenting wondrous images of benefits but with little acknowledgment of the costs involved. Once mired in their grasp, the individual becomes bound and tied in indebtedness, an indebtedness that limits options and strangles choices.

Having gone through an archaic and defunct education system, high school and college students, college graduates and most adults are largely illiterate ---

- illiterate in critical thinking,

- illiterate in clear self-expression,

- illiterate in civics and how the government works or is supposed to work,

- and financially illiterate.

We now have generations that are sitting ducks for the predators, and predators there are all around.

A Sitting Duck is Liable to Get Cooked

Chapter 10:   THE PHOENIX RISES

If you have read this far, you probably have a rather somber outlook on college and university education. And you should.

Like pulling back the curtain of the *Wizard of Oz* screen, it is essential to see who, what and why are pulling the strings, punching the buttons. What I have presented is an unfavorable perspective on today's college education.

Before you enlist in 4-6 years, which come with heavy financial costs and with lost income opportunity costs and an increasingly questionable return-on-investment, it is important that the prospective college student see the downside of today's higher education.

There are many out there cheerleading for a college education.

- There are the colleges themselves who survive and thrive on the body count. They need tuition-paying students in order to keep the doors open, even when the tuition-paying student is indenturing themselves to the usury interest rate loans of student debt.

- There are the traditionalists who assert the past belief that a college education is the only way to get ahead in life, to be successful and to be fulfilled.

- There are government agencies that encourage high school students to take the next step into college with a flurry of statistics that might be relevant for the present, more so perhaps for the past, but questionable for the future.

- There are parents and peers who insist that college is the requisite step in the chronological unfolding of a student's life.

As if in chorus, different entities will spout out the pros of a college education and downplay any negatives.

Are they delusional? Are they trying to have you buy into their illusions?

The old and current models of higher education are DEAD

College and university schooling no longer effectively fulfill the promise of higher education. The development of critical thinking, the consideration of the varied perspectives on a topic, and the rational analysis of a particular topic are no longer the hallmark of a college education.

Learning essential skills for the intended career path from a college education no longer is the outcome from a four to six year enlistment in higher education.

College education has moved from a profession to yet another business, and a business where the consumer is king but at very substantial costs.

Today's college education can be seen largely as a form of warehousing --- entertaining students for four to six years before continuing on with yet more education in graduate school or entering a labor force that is winnowing down to a precious few.

Should we despair?

We should be disheartened by what has become of higher education. We need not despair if we would remove the blinders from our eyes and look with peripheral vision regarding options and alternatives to the traditional higher education model.

As I have pointed out through the pages of this book,

the times they are a'changing

With the technology of the Information Age, we have more information at our fingertips than at any time in the past. There are greater options and alternatives to gain the knowledge and understanding of the tools to develop our skill set than ever before.

We just have to recognize the opportunities of these times.

The Internet has provided a key to unlock the vast wealth of information, knowledge and learning at our disposal. Much of the requisite information on the Internet is free. Some of the learning on the Internet comes with a cost. The Internet opens the door to being anywhere and everywhere and still capable of receiving the transmissions of teaching skills, developing the mind, and increasing the knowledge base.

We are no longer dependent upon the brick and mortar. Requisite attendance at a physical college campus is no longer necessary to gain skills or even accomplish a graduation degree.

Increasingly, colleges and universities are offering degree programs online. Although in its infancy with all the growing pains of a new model or a new way of doing things, online degree programs provide the teaching of courses that their on-site programs offer on the college campus.

For working individuals, an online degree program offers the student greater flexibility than the classroom attendance, for it provides the student the ability to take the class and learn the requisite knowledge on their own terms, at their own pace and at their own preferable times.

While there are online college degree programs from undergraduate through graduate degrees, the question also arises as to whether a college degree is as necessary as in times past.

Many of the courses to attain a college degree seem irrelevant, often fluff, and offered primarily to entertain the student.

Fluff courses are often associated with the liberal arts education. As noted before, most of the *'teachers'* in the humanities steer towards a very Liberal viewpoint. These *'teachers'* are often social justice warriors masquerading as true teachers. They spout their party line, demean opportunity as some sort of unjustified *'privilege'*, and instead of building students up and educating them, often guilt their students and shame them to indoctrinate them into their own narrow viewpoint. This is not what education, and especially higher education, is all about.

A large number of these *'teachers'* on college campuses have spent little, if any, significant time in the real world. On the contrary, they have largely been coddled within the walls of their college campuses with the *'opportunity'* of doing life on a theoretical basis rather than a hands-on involvement. It is all well and good to pontificate and project one's opinions as empirical facts, but theory and practice can be totally divorced from one another, with one tending toward the more subjective, the practical being more objective.

What to do for a student who is looking to further their studies, who wishes to gain greater understanding, and who wants to hone their skills to successfully take their place in society?

While the college experience can provide a phenomenal arena for socialization, a place where one can interact with greater diversity, people of foreign nations, people from different cultural backgrounds, and people from varied economic strata; the college experience comes with huge cost:

a. financially with the exorbitant expenses of tuition, fees and living costs; expenses that may take much of a lifetime to repay.

b. the loss of income potential during those college years; future income then being docked by paying off the student loan debt both taken on for their college expenses and the accrued interest compounded on the debt principal.

c. indoctrination into a mindset that might work in a theoretical world but has little applicability to the real world.

d. an education where the bar has been lowered to such a degree that basic learning skills are NOT developed, only a negative attitude of all that is wrong in the world with little consideration of all that is right in the world.

Education from primary through secondary through college has become largely a pass along.

you pay your money, you get your prize

everyone gets a ribbon or a trophy just for showing up and participating

Apart from online studies, whether drawing upon *'free'* information or pay for courses, there are other ways of gaining the relevant skill set for your career and potential career opportunities.

Some colleges offer a co-op program with studies in college counterbalanced by hands-on work in the student's field of study. Not only can the student get income from their work, but they gain the hands-on work experience complementing their college studies. The income from work can pay towards tuition and offset college costs.

In years past, and still a significant factor, is the concept of apprenticeship, whereby hands-on helps the apprentice to develop the skills to master their craft. By doing so, theoretical studies are replaced by real world situations.

Theory is all well and good but it is only that --

theoretical

No theory can take into account all the exigencies of a real life situation. Theory can give a framework and a template and provide general rules, but theory is not always successfully applicable to real world issues. Experience always beats theory, and yet so many college *'teachers'* are theorists, teachers who were students and have stayed solely on the education track without getting their hands dirty in real term conditions.

Companies such as Google and angel investors like Peter Thiel have indicated that they would prefer to hire pre-college employees. Their sentiment is that the potential employee has not been inculcated into a mindset that deflates individual creativity and originality but instills instead a dumbing down and a numbing of the creative self.

Already, in incipient ways, higher education is changing. While for some students, college education is a country club experience with all sorts of amenities and recreational opportunities and courses that are little more than popular pastimes, for other students who are truly committed to the love of learning and a desire to develop their skill set for the real world, there are alternatives to the traditional brick and mortar college education.

Technology has rocked our world!

And it will continue to do so

If you decide that you want to have, must have, a college education, proceed with caution, with your eyes wide open and your ear to the track of innovation in higher education.

If you decide you want the college experience on campus, consider doing your first two years at a community college. The expenses are far less. You can get your core requirements out of the way. And you can transfer after your first two years to a college where you finish your college education and from which you get your college degree.

My purpose in writing this book has been to make you aware of the downsides associated with today's higher education.

College is not what it has been, and you will have to decide whether you choose to believe that college is for lunkheads or whether a traditional college education is for you.

Until there is truly a radical transformation of higher education, the present day college experience affirms the concept that

College IS for Lunkheads